Tom Murphy's plays have been performed throughout the world, including London's West End, the Royal Court, the Almeida Theatre and the Donmar Warehouse. His career has been markedly associated with the famous Abbey Theatre in Dublin, where eighteen of his plays have been performed. His plays include *A Whistle in the Dark*, *The Gigli Concert*, *Famine*, *The Morning After Optimism*, *The Sanctuary Lamp*, *The Patriot Game*, *The Blue Macushla*, *The Patriot Game*, *Too Late for Logic*, *Conversations on a Homecoming*, and *Bailegangaire*. He is a member of the Irish Academy of Letters and lives in Dublin. *The Seduction of Morality* is his first novel.

THE SEDUCTION
OF MORALITY

Tom Murphy

An *Abacus* Book

First published in Great Britain by Little, Brown and Company 1994
This edition published by Abacus 1995
Reprinted 1996, 1997

A CIP catalogue record for this book
is available from the British Library.

ISBN 0 349 10617 7

Printed and bound in Great Britain by Clays Ltd, St Ives plc

Abacus
A Division of
Little, Brown and Company (UK)
Brettenham House
Lancaster Place
London WC2E 7EN

CONTENTS

I

THE PAST

When Vera was three, when Tom came along, she was sent to live with her widowed maternal grandmother, Mom, in the country. The system of fostering-out was not unusual in the past. And, in this case, Mom had a farm.

The land was mostly let out in grazing, but there was plenty of work to be done. There was a cow, That Lady, to be milked, and a churn, and there was sometimes a pig which Mom killed and cured. Vera was given the bladder, a kind of early balloon. And there were hens and ducks as well as the kitchen garden, which was also an orchard of sorts with a few leaning apple trees, a cat called Robber and St Peter, a cock, who chased the hens to make them lay. The nearest neighbour was a quarter of a mile up the road, the village two miles beyond that.

Mom had another occupation and Vera sometimes accompanied

her on her trips. She was a midwife. Vera watched her ministering. The foot movements, the large round body swaying, hands weaving to find deliberation, the eyes appearing as if not to as much as even blink before the new-born arrived. Then all would be still for a moment in frowning wonder, and then she would say: 'Now! Naked we came into the world!'

She shaved and laid out the dead, undressed and dressed them again. The same foot movements, the same intensity until, job done, stillness again, frowning wonder.

And when Vera would strip and stand two feet in the basin on the kitchen floor, to wash in the way that Mom had shown her, she would hold her breath at her own nakedness. And Mom, seated by the hearth, would nod solemnly her understanding and respect.

People said that Mom was cross, meaning difficult; some said fierce, that she drove people away. But she and Vera got on well. Vera was a quiet child: that suited Mom. She didn't mind in the slightest the journey for the can of porter once a week, could carry it without spilling a drop, then running to the dresser for the mug and when, after a few, Mom laughed, Vera too would throw back her head and feel the exhilaration of hearing her own and Mom's laughter filling the thatched house. Mom suited Vera too. And when, sometimes, Mom cried and hugged Vera so tightly that it hurt, Vera understood. Naked we came into the world.

Then Uncle Willie returned from San Jose. He had a glass eye and he carried a mirror with him everywhere. Vera was fascinated by him. Nevertheless, as Mom's son, his presence claimed the farm. Twenty-six acres, three roods, nineteen perches. And Vera was recalled home.

But her regret in leaving Mom was more than tempered by her excitement. She often thought of her family as the perfect place or state of happiness; even the secret guilt of her unworthiness was important to her; through her mother and her father, her brother

Tom, and she now had two younger sisters, she would be saved, she would belong. The thought continued into later life, until she was thirty-eight, in fact.

II

THE FAMILY

Vera arrived home from New York in a modest brown hatchback. Her mother had died suddenly. The size and colour of the car were thought out: a nod to thrift, a gesture to conformity.

'Is that yours?' said her youngest sister Mary Jane. 'Did you bring it *all* the way from America?'

'No, it's rented.'

Tom sucked in air through his smile. 'Put it in the yard, sure, Vera, why don't you?' he said, glancing about to see if there was anyone on the busy square. 'Where it'll be safe, sure.'

Her middle sister, too, Marcia, looked alarmed at the little Renault. Then she turned her swollen eyes on Vera. 'You'll never see her now,' she said, 'she's coffined.'

After the funeral, mourners and sympathizers assembled in the lobby and lounge bar for the ritual drinks. Vera was not very good in this type of gathering and tended to stand back, leaving

4

the hosting to her youngest sister, to her brother, her sister-in-law Caitriona and to Miss Rooney, the manageress. Marcia, the middle sister, was still stricken.

'You remember Mrs Brown and Mrs Lawlor, sure, don't you, Vera?' said her brother Tom and then went off in search of others.

'And you're still in America,' they said. Neither statement nor question.

'Yes.'

'Now.'

'New York you're in I suppose all the time.'

'Yes.'

'Look at that now.'

She never could get the hang of this kind of conversation. She could do with other company. Behind her smile she felt her social lacking. She could almost envy Marcia's state. She looked round for Mom but her grandmother was nowhere to be seen. She had had only a few words with Mom at the graveside. And when she asked her friend, Finbar Reilly, back for a drink when he sympathized with her, he said, 'The hotel? Nix-nix-nix, Vera! A fella like me to go approaching a place like that could be arrested for loitering.' She could do with another drink.

'It's expensive over there,' they said.

'Quite expensive.'

'But you're doing well.'

'Quite well.'

Tom brought her another company and he winked secret encouragement at her to humour them. Miss Rooney brought another tray of drinks, and Caitriona brought another.

Father Billy was a blessing. He laughed and clapped his hands at almost everything. His waisted black overcoat emphasized the width of his shoulders, the size of his chest. And his white silk scarf. He was a gift. But then they got linked to the next circle.

'Are priests *really* necessary to our salvation?' said The Greek, who was a brother-in-law of Vera's. He had several law degrees.

'I don't know what you mean, like, Henry boy,' said Father Billy.

'Be sincere, Billy,' said The Greek. He was the tallest man in the room.

'I don't have the time, like – not like some people!'

And Father Billy had to be off – alas for Vera, because the attention, she knew, would shortly turn on her.

'If you're not in the hotel trade over there, what are you in?' said Mike Hammer, the auctioneer. Small towns, like children, have a genius for nicknames.

'I'm a call-girl,' said Vera.

They laughed. The funeral party was coming to life. They would not believe her.

She explained. 'A hooker, a prostitute.'

They admired her daring and you could see in the pause before they laughed again that the idea had its attractions, but such a thing was impossible. She was from the town – the Imperial Hotel! – home for her mother's funeral.

'Vera is a feminist,' said The Greek, 'asserting in analogy her protest of woman's lot in the social order.'

'Man is a slave and woman is the slave of a slave!' said the young solicitor who was new to the town, quoting someone, though not quite knowing what he meant by it. But it too went down well.

'Be the hokies!' said Mike Hammer.

But you could see them reconsidering. Their wit, perhaps, was rash. After all, word had it a few years back that Mick Sweeney, the Dublin Road, was doing live performances in Soho and, though Vera did not look like a whore, there had always been something about her manner.

'But, all the same, what're yeh doing over there, seriously?'

'Let's drink another toast to the dead,' said Vera. 'Heigh-ho!'

At the end of the evening, Vera asked Miss Rooney could she, instead of sleeping in number 14, the room that had been prepared for her, sleep in her old room in the attic.

'I understand,' said Miss Rooney.

Next morning it became known that Vera had inherited the Imperial Hotel, the family home, lock, stock and barrel and was returning to the States that afternoon. It was clear that her brother, sisters and in-laws were surprised, to say the least of it, by this turn of events. They found it difficult to think. An early lunch was arranged.

Vera had known for a dozen years of her inheritance. She hadn't wanted it; it was forced on her. Her father had nearly died intestate and the confusion that could have ensued was averted only at the last moment. However, the family had been alerted to the dangers of dying without making a will and its attentions were turned on Uncle Brendan, who was three years older than Vera's father and a bachelor. On the fear of sudden death Uncle Brendan came to live at the hotel and, shortly afterwards, Vera's mother assembled the family around him in the upstairs sitting-room for the share-out of his property.

Tom got Uncle Brendan's house on the hill; Marcia, who had recently married The Greek, the barrister, got the Shamrock Ballroom and Mary Jane got the Capitol Cinema and the Magnet next door to it. All that remained now of Uncle Brendan's estate was the dormant The Wool Stores and this had been ear-marked for Vera. Vera hung back. Her uncle's hanging lower lip and watery eyes were upsetting her and, though her mother took her shoulder to pull her forward to the table, Vera resisted and said she did not want anything.

Tom got The Wool Stores too.

All the recipients of Uncle Brendan's largesse were obligated to their mother and made private financial arrangements with her. Because the arrangements were never properly honoured and because, in Tom's case, a single penny of the nine hundred extra for the bonus of his getting The Wool Stores was never handed over, and because their mother considered Vera to be a fool, Vera was paraded suddenly one day to the family solicitor's where, in a fit of pique, the Imperial was signed over to her in a deed.

If Vera's inheritance came as a surprise to them, that was their mother's fault. Vera had so little interest in the place, then as now, it never crossed her mind to mention it. Why her mother had not done so is a matter for speculation. She had become an alcoholic; in fact, a fall down the stairs had precipitated her death. In her final years she had taken to roaming the corridors late at night, laughing at and abusing the sleeping guests, and so had, probably, forgotten the whole business; or, though drink-crazed, if she did remember it, pique lingered to take a last harsh laugh to the grave.

Caitriona, who was Tom's wife, and her three children, and Declan, who was Mary Jane's husband, called in to say goodbye to Vera. They couldn't stay to lunch. They had to get back, they said. There was no sign of The Greek. Vera was glad that they did not stay. She interpreted the departure of her in-laws as tact: they did not wish to be present at a function that had been arranged to enable her to hand over the hotel. She never led and so she waited for them to bring the subject up but, at best, only oblique references were being made to it.

'Lookit!' said Tom, laughing heartily and rubbing his hands. 'Will we all relax now, for the love of God, and enjoy a good lunch, because that's what I'm going to do! I don't know and I don't care who is prop'ietor or prop'ietess of this establishment but I'm flaming hungry! Where would you like to sit, Vera? I'm paying for this meal and I'd like to know who's going to stop me! I haven't a care in the world presently, thank God, we gave our mother a good send-off and that's the main thing!'

Academically, the family was not a distinguished one and, here, Tom was supreme. He failed both the Intermediate and Leaving Certificates and for a time it was thought that he would have to enter politics or the priesthood. At the age of twenty, however, he matriculated. Then, acting on the advice of a mentor to forgo university, he used the achievement instead to apply for the Civil Service, any department. Though it was insufficient qualification he had the pull of two parliamentary secretaries and was accepted into the Department of Industry and Commerce. He was now Weights-and-Measures Man for the area.

He took up the carver and whistled in short bursts. 'Breast I'm sure for you, Vera!'

He was thirty-four. He lived in the house on the hill overlooking the town with his wife Caitriona, whom he called Little Treasure, and their three children. He still had The Wool Stores. He had acquired a half-share in The Sacré Coeur, a guest-house, in partnership with his solicitor: sound enough in a Grade B way but could go nowhere else as far as he could see, so, all in good time, let his solicitor buy him out. He invested in gilts and post office savings, and speculated a little in oil-rigs. They mightn't find oil but they needed the rigs to find that out. He was a respected member of several organizations in the town of a commercial, cultural, church and charitable nature. He made all the arrangements for his mother's funeral, including the car that collected Mom from the country, both days, and home again immediately afterwards. He visited Mom regularly and brought her sweets, warned her about crooks and advised of the dangers of letting grazing in any form but the eleven-month system; and he had seen to it, last year, that he would inherit the farm when she died. He took a drink and could carry a tune on the piano. He wore his father's white star which was of subtle size in his Sunday lapel, the symbol of a clean tongue. And he never told a lie. On advice from one of his spiritual advisors he wrote little notes to Little Treasure: he discovered her several times recently when he got home, sitting under the radio in the kitchen, looking at a spot on the floor. He knew all along about Vera; he did not have to remind himself of precedents of behaviour in her so-called reticent nature, else how could she have out-manoeuvred him with his mother, trying to do him out of his birthright, a man? Which did not mean of course rubbing her the wrong way. It required thought; there was Mary Jane to guard against and he hoped that Little Treasure was not going to give him any trouble while he worked it out. He was proud of his morals; he loved them.

'Wasn't it nice that the Bishop attended?' said Mary Jane.

'A-a-a-w!' said Tom, crouched over the table, enthusiasm freezing his every movement. 'Wasn't it?' he said hoarsely. 'Man dear alive!' Then he said, recovering, 'But he was very fond of her. Aidan, sure! The Bishop! Did you not know that, Vera? Oh, very, very fond of Mother. It was possibly the Mayo connection.' He looked round to see if they wanted him, at this stage, to elaborate on the connection.

'Could you hand us over the peas?' said Mary Jane.

'Lookit,' Tom said, handing over the peas, 'the fact that Bishop Aidan attended would've given a great rise to Mother, it would've suited her down to the ground!'

'Are you all right, Marcy?' said Vera.

'I don't care,' said Marcia, or perhaps she said, 'It's not fair,' crying into her napkin.

Her eyes were still enlarged; in fact she looked bewildered. She was pregnant again, The Greek, the barrister husband, never practised, didn't get up until two o'clock in the day and dancehalls were a thing of the past. The Shamrock was a white elephant; even at site-value it was hopelessly situated; it was rented to a gobshite for virtually nothing.

Tom saw Vera glance at her watch. Vera saw that Tom had seen her and she smiled apologetically. Tom turned on Marcia.

'Lookit here!' he said sternly. 'Marcia, are you listening to me? Whatever you said back there, how dare you! How-flaming-dare-you! Are you listening?' And when she nodded that she was he continued more kindly. 'How dare you, man dear alive! I'll have your life! Don't you know that every tear shed for the departed is a hole through the wings of an angel? Man dear alive sure, don't you know Mother is in heaven now?' Tears came to his eyes and, addressing his plate, he said, 'The woman was a saint, sure.'

'Pass us down the bread sauce,' said Mary Jane to him. Mary Jane was the baby in the family.

> Bide your time, your worst transgression
> Were to strike and strike in vain;
> He whose hand would smite oppression
> Must not need to strike again.

A jingle-poem from school that appealed to her. It made business sense. Only once had she acted precipitately and it had nearly been her undoing. She nearly married The Greek.

Unlike her sisters – Tom was in-between in size – Mary Jane took after her father's side of the family and so was only a little over five feet tall. When it became known in the town that she and The Greek were serious, someone remarked, 'She'll be too small for him, sure,' and, in the manner of small towns, this became a catch-phrase. She was present herself when the remark was passed one evening in the lounge bar. So was her father. Sipping from a glass of water behind the counter, as was his wont, and looking out on the Square. He chewed his food thirteen times before swallowing: that kind of private man. 'She'll be too small for him, sure!' Her father heard it also. She never saw him angry, nor did he appear angry now. He put down his glass, thought, then came out easily from under the counter, straightened himself and said evenly, 'Would she be tall enough for him, Murphy, with five thousand pounds under each heel?'

He barred Murphy – and indicated to the entire group present that it was their choice to follow Murphy out the door if they wished to do so – for life from the Imperial Hotel. Then he returned to his place behind the counter, lifted his glass of water and, whilst drinking from it, turned his eyes in Mary Jane's direction and cocked a finger. She had been rescued from the brink.

Shrewdly, she had unloaded the Capitol Cinema on a returned emigrant and sold the Magnet to a local within eighteen months of coming legally into them. She could have done better by the Magnet had she held it but, as her GP, in whom she confided, said, 'That is no skin off your back now.'

Simultaneously, she was courting Declan Mansfield who was healthily disgusted in his role as a bank clerk. He was five feet seven and from the start he called her MJ. She recognized an achievable ambition in his eye and he was a more-than-average amateur carpenter. They married, lived in a small flat for a year over Crisham's pub, then they bought Crisham's, sold the licence – there were twenty-eight other pubs in the town – converted it into a supermarket – Declan did a lot of the conversion himself – called *Daze and Nytes*. The Greek coined the name for them and The Greek it was who performed the opening ceremony. 'Daze,' he said, 'because of a dream distracted in young Declan's eye; Nytes, because I know from experience Mary Jane to be an insomniac,' which was mortifying for a moment. But, 'Nyet!' said The Greek. 'Hold it! Let me rephrase. *Daze and Nytes* because of Zeal's generous, inexpectant look in this selfless young couple, undaunted in the thought of protracted, shoulder-length hours of social service pro bono publico,' which was published in the paper.

There were times when you couldn't help but like The Greek; still, she'd be ashamed to be turned into a baby elephant in the eyes of the town by him, like Marcia, every other year.

Though not rich enough to have a child, Mary Jane and Declan were prospering. But *Daze and Nytes*, no matter what they did, was effectively only eleven hundred and fifty square feet and the Dublin crowd were scouting about. If only they could get The Wool Stores off Tom without alerting him. They were very much a team and hand-in-hand they sometimes stepped its frontage in the dark. Seventy-five feet. Two floors: four thousand square feet. The rear fronting on to the old shambles: a natural car park. And it would make you scream: it was just sitting there. If only they could get it, hold it for a couple of years until they were ready to develop it – thus, and also, stopping the Dublin crowd moving in; let them scout and shunt about then anyway they liked – and sell *Daze and Nytes* to the North of Ireland crowd that didn't know where to run with its money, they'd be on top of the wheel. But, bide your time, your worst trangression were to strike and strike in vain.

'Is there no way at all, at all you could stay on for a few days?' She was thirty-one, two months older than Declan, exactly to the day.

'I'm booked,' said Vera.

'Because you're more than welcome,' said Marcia.

'Oh!' said Tom. 'Oh – but did you see your man yesterday?'

'Ah, that's a pity,' said Mary Jane to Vera.

'Your man, your man,' said Tom, 'in the grey gaberdine! Man dear alive, a near-albino, bejakers! Well, d'you know who he is now?'

'When will you be home again?' said Mary Jane.

'I don't know,' said Vera apologetically. 'But time is getting on.' It was becoming unlikely that the problem of her inheritance would be resolved today.

She was hoping to make a quick run out to Mom's and spend half an hour there. Then she would have nearly a hundred miles to drive, return the hatchback and check in at the airport by six o'clock. She had a headache, a hangover from the night before. To her, Mary Jane was being strangely demure, not at all her normal, impatient, businesslike self; Marcia's contributions only seemed to make Marcia more clumsy, red and bloated than she really was, then becoming transfixed in a new alarm like a puffed child attending a circus; and every time she looked at Tom he looked elsewhere, renewing bursts of information about people she did not even know and the complications of their lineage. She drank too much when ill at ease and she hoped she had not been too big of an embarrassment to them last night at the wake.

She was thirty-seven and only too painfully aware she was the eldest: the thought fed her insecurity. All her life she could not take the lead that she knew was her responsibility. She loved them, but right from the time she returned from the country, the nine and a half years she had spent with Mom, she was shy of them. And they gave her all sorts of chances.

The day her father was buried her mother assembled them in the upstairs sitting-room where his personal effects, the little things he kept about him, were laid out on the table. Each of them was called forward to take something as a keepsake. Vera was called first on this occasion. She was very touched – she still cherished the honour – and she knew that her mother was both testing her and trying to train her, but she could not overcome her diffidence and, looking at her mother with tear-filled eyes of gratitude, she shook her head. Tom selected the white star and the half-hunter; Marcia, next in age to Tom, took the tie-pin, pioneer-pin, studs, two fountain pens, a packet of Rennies and the rosary beads; Mary Jane, the embossed leather wallet, said to be intact. Vera then asked could she have her father's pipe.

But there is a contradiction at the heart of everything and Vera was not always so passive. Earlier, the year that Uncle Willie died, the children were told that they could not attend the funeral in the country. That night, while her parents were away, Vera robbed her money-box of every penny it contained with a knife, bought sweets for Finbar Reilly and took him to the pictures at the Capitol.

And there was the secret of her growing interest in Morality. The village school that she attended when living with Mom was straightforward as compared with the convent in the town. Here, the emphasis was not on the Catechism but on Morality. In her first year she was thrown in at the deep end. The Retreat.

'The devil is a person,' said the Redemptorist Father. 'He is usually a grown-up and a smiler. But he is skilled in his disguises and you may find him in a boy of ten-and-a-half.'

The Redemptorist Father had spent time in the continent of Africa but the small convent chapel gave an intimacy to what he was imparting as to induce alarming alternating emotions. Cold fear of the smiling devil made the eyes dilate, hot fear made the eyelids heavy again. Worse still, confessions were heard in the actual classroom, in daylight, where the blackboard was and everything. The smell of chalk and ink was heavier than incense.

'Do you have a boyfriend, my child?'

He held his breath at her hesitation, an evasion. The matter was of such burning gravity he could not even look at her. 'Do you have a boyfriend?' he whispered in his hopeless manner.

'Tom,' and she clapped her mouth shut, but too late: she had already whispered it. And it was a stupid thing to say that your brother was your boyfriend but that was what she had answered to the same question from Mom one time.

'What?'

'Tom.' She had whispered it again; she couldn't stop herself. The Redemptorist nearly looked at her but didn't and she thought he was going to give up. 'Tom.' She whispered it again. Somehow, she did not want to let the Redemptorist down.

'Do you meet?'

'Yes.'

'Do you kiss him?'

'Yes.'

'Does he kiss you?'

'Yes.'

'What?'

'He does.'

'How often?'

'Birthdays.'

'Yes?'

'And Christmas.'

'Is the kissing passionate?'

His head was unmoving, grey, cropped and bowed to his chest, his lips were hanging open, eyes screwed upwards, fixed on the map of Ireland on the other wall, his hands in the slits of his soutane.

It was very frightening in an exciting way and she kept whispering yes and nodding her head. Hypnotizing.

'Is it what?' she whispered.

'Passionate, on the mouth.'

'Yes.'

'The open mouth?'

'Yes.'

'With the tongue?'

'The what?'

'The open mouth, the tongue.'

'Yes.'

'Are there immodest touches?'

'Yes.'

'Above or below the waist?'

'Yes.'

'Which? Above?'

'Yes.'

'Below?'

'Yes.'

'Does he expose himself?'

'He does.'

'Does he shed seed?'

'Yes.'

'Aw-a-www!' He groaned, a moan, hollow, a sound as from the bowels of the earth. Then he said, sorrowfully, 'Little girls have been caught out before. They go to hell for all eternity where, naked, they are dipped into the fire.'

It was shortly after this, before she was fourteen, that Vera became interested in Finbar Reilly from the Punjab, that is, the New Estate. In her affair with Finbar, the contradiction in her passive nature showed itself at its most perverse, obdurate to advice, pleas and threats.

'Well,' said Vera, closing her knife and fork, and the others leaned forward and fixed on her, 'that's that.'

She had to be going, she was running late. She didn't even have time to drive out and see Mom. She had a word with Miss Rooney, who gave her a set of keys, and she collected her bag.

'Miss Rooney,' said Vera, 'will look after the place until – Heigh-ho!' Until they were all recovered from their mother's death and could sort out their minds.

They went to the yard where the small brown hatchback was parked.

'I'll write,' said Mary Jane into Vera's ear as she kissed her.

Tom opened the porch doors and held them.

Give my love to Mom said Vera.

Tom told her not to worry about a thing. He told her that he knew a teacher, a Kilkenny man, married to one of Patrick Hession's daughters, Evelyn, who taught science in the Newcastle Tech and swore by Renaults. He told her that he would be writing to her, please God, and God speed.

Marcia, unsure that her eyes could contain themselves further, remained inside, watching from the window.

Vera circled the Square to turn. Finbar Reilly was standing by the monument, as she knew he would be, in his shabby clothes. But he was shaven and Brylcreemed. He smiled, winked and saluted her. He was proud of the romance they had together twenty-three years ago. She turned the hatchback off the Square on to the Dublin Road. She was glad to be going back but she was sorry she had not had a sit-down with Mom. She was sorry, too, she hadn't had a drink with Finbar. It was possible that he was still a virgin. Next time.

III

LETTERS FROM HOME

This time she was driving a Merc. Extremes seemed to suit her. The unapologetic directness of New York, the elemental simplicity of life in the country with Mom. But how to deal with the mean of the town?

She left the Dublin suburbs behind and began to meet the countryside. It was May but the country looked confused, trying to be all things. The ash trees had not broken and the slanting light at every bend was a nuisance. It was all too variable, too clever. Still, the Merc was a blessing: silver no-nonsense that knew what it had to do and got on with it; its independent will cut through the confusion. She began to celebrate the authority of the car, her frown lifted, to forget herself, almost. The punctuations at ten-mile intervals, the small towns she had to traverse, this one like the last, with a Central, Grand, Castle, Royal, an Imperial hotel reminding her of home and making her gulp in sighs at the thought of her family. And she doubted that the rented Merc would suit them either.

There was going to be an auction. Surprising. But that was what they recommended. They suggested that it would not be necessary for her to come home. Fair enough. But then, astonishing, 'PS. Mom dead.'

She had had letters from them all. Well, strictly speaking not from Marcia, from Norman, Marcia's and The Greek's eldest. A whole series of letters.

Tom never saw anything like the Indian summer they were having, how hot was it in New York? His Little Treasure's nerves were playing her up again, she was feeling house-bound, but this was only natural when you considered her highly specialized education and diploma. But this in turn was affecting Martina, who was at that age; it was feared that Joe was possibly dyslexic but thank God for Aisling who was a little doll. And miscellaneous information of a local nature. The entire family was saying tell us how on earth are you, Vera, at all.

Mary Jane wrote just a few lines. You'd hardly recognize the Imperial the way it was deteriorating, a month exactly to the day since their mother was buried; Declan himself had commented on it. He had called in yesterday, 3.00 pm, only to find Miss Rooney entertaining two members of her family in the upstairs sitting-room. She had gone up herself, 4.00 pm, to find them similarly ensconced. In confidence at this stage what could they do to help Vera at all? Would she give them an idea?

'Dear Aunty Vera I'll be eleven years old next Sunday. Dad is in St Pats. I hope the baby is going to be a boy. Lots and lots of love from Norman. XOXOXOX. P.S. And lots and lots of love from Mum. XOX.'

A mild winter followed the Indian summer and further letters asked for climatic comparisons.

Tom had been offered promotion, he had a family to rear and everyone was passing him out but he was thinking he wouldn't flaming take it. What did she think? He would like to think that the humble little town of Grange was and always would be, no

19

matter what, if he could help it at all, the place where he'd draw breath. Caitriona, his Little Treasure, was fine. She was a great little manager and you'd smile if you saw how pleased as punch she was when he dug out her diploma and nailed it to the wall the other night. What do you think of that? He had ordered a white marble headstone to put over his father and mother, he didn't care what anyone said but the old one was mean. He bore his father's name no matter what and it was the least he could do as the only son. And did she know that Mary Jane and Declan Mansfield had a set of keys to the hotel?

Mary Jane wrote about the new extension built in the forties by Turlough O'Driscoll, a contractor who skimped to the point of criminality – Daddy often confided his troubles in Mary Jane as a child – using more actual cement bags than the cement they contained, an old trick, in the construction, as well as half-rotten timber riddled with woodworm; it always leaked. Well, you should see it now, and she doubted it would stand the winter. Miss Rooney was feeding her family, relations and half the town in the hotel; Mary Jane would like to see a balance sheet my dear at the end of the financial year, 5th April. Did Vera give permission to Tom or did she know that he now had a trailer permanently parked in the yard? In confidence, had Vera considered power-of-attorney?

It was time to talk flaming business. Did Vera know that things were disappearing from the hotel, was that what Tom's father raised the name O'Toole up for? That nice little gilt mirror on the half-landing and the little silver statue of the Blessed Virgin out of his mother's room that meant so much to his mother. He was fit to be tied. That you'd think the Mansfields were now sleeping in the hotel, that he knew every jot and tittle about Declan Mansfield and the Mansfield clan, that he didn't want to as much as even mention the name Mansfield. Bluntly speaking he wouldn't say that he was very but he'd say that he was interested, which was only natural, in the hotel and what he was proposing was this: had everyone forgotten that his Little Treasure was a highly qualified woman and had a diploma in home economics which was more than could be said for Miss Rooney who was patently mismanaging the place and impertinent into the bargain, or Mary Jane Mansfield for that matter. Had everyone flaming forgotten that? And what he was proposing was that he move his Little Treasure out, what could be more natural, into the hotel and let them take it up between them then from there. Man dear alive her affectionate brother.

Mary Jane. Did Vera know that items were disappearing whole-sale from the Imperial; did she know that her sister-in-law Caitriona O'Toole's drink problem was only second to her brother-in-law's, The Greek's? Did she know that her brother Tom had tried to get rid of Miss Rooney and that Miss Rooney had only been dissuaded, just, by Declan and herself from going to the tribunal and the labour courts? Not that she could find anything whatsoever in Miss Rooney to support. Did she know that tinkers were now being served in the hotel and you know what that leads to. Honestly Mary Jane was not getting a wink. So, had Vera thought since of power-of-attorney, if not to Mary Jane herself then to Declan who was neutral in all matters. Give-us-your-instructions. I do wish you would write, Vera.

Mary Jane's rebuke was just and Vera knew it. The place indeed could collapse or fall so deeply into debt through mismanagement that a bank would take it over. The members of her family were very busy people in their lives; she was the one, yet again, falling down on her duty and upsetting them. And it wasn't as if she was busy; on the contrary, things had become incredibly slack. And Christmas was on the horizon. And the reason why she had not given them instructions was not because she hated writing; no. She certainly was no hand at putting pen to paper but she had been giving the matter of the hotel some consideration of late. Her thinking, as follows, gave her a headache and made her squirm with embarrassment in her 10th Avenue apartment.

The day of the lunch, yes, the day following her mother's funeral, she would have signed anything, unconditionally, if any one of them or all of them had produced anything for her to sign. But that was then. Now, on reflection, couldn't that grand, unconditional gesture be interpreted as a clever tactic of buying her way into the family's affections by making them eternally grateful to her?

She thought further, building on this.

Shortly after Mary Jane and Declan bought Crisham's pub and were turning it into *Daze and Nytes*, Vera was home from New York and Mary Jane and Declan took her on a proud tour of their new home and premises. Not wanting to liquidize – or was it freeze? Whichever, that kind of word – some percentage of their assets, and not wanting to or wanting to capitalize – exploit? – the advantages of taking out a loan, and several other considerations, they 'grabbed time by the forelock' and managed very cleverly to assemble the ninety-two and a half thousand that they needed to buy Crisham's and, on this careless reckoning, Vera felt that the Imperial Hotel on the Square had to be worth as much as Crisham's pub in Cairn Place.

Now, ideally, what she would like to see happen was that one of them, Tom, or all of them, should say to her, I want it, or we want it, here's ninety thousand pounds. Or fifty or forty or thirty or twenty. But preferably ninety. To which she would say, give me ten. And ten, she told herself, would keep the matter – the transaction! – on a proper footing. After all, things were becoming very complicated. Ten simplified everything. They might even consider it a very wise business gesture on her part and be impressed.

But she knew she was being dishonest. A certain type of lying was acceptable, was even desirable at times, but lying to herself? She was thirty-seven, pushing thirty-eight, business was terrible, Christmas was coming, ten thousand would guarantee the roof over her head for five years. £10,000? She had no right to it. Not only that, and not only was she being selfish, she was thinking dangerously: it could further remove her from them; it could be seen as an act of selling herself out of the family. And that was the very last thing she wanted.

The thought of asking her family for ten thousand pounds made her squirm. If by some happy accident one of them, or all of them, came up with the same bright idea of making her the offer, it would be a different matter. Heigh-ho! All of them would have to sit it out for a little longer.

She received a Christmas card from Norman, made by himself. It showed a yellow sun rising between two green hills. The yellow rays fanning upwards cut a swathe through a dark blue sky that seemed to fall away on either side from the warm light. The white dots were sheep grazing on the hills, the smudges in brown were cattle or bushes. Up near the top the lines of crayon were interrupted to create a box, and in the box was the printed message, WAKE UP TO A NICE DAY, in red. Inside he had written, 'To Aunty Vera. Happy Christmas. Hope you have a nice Christmas. No brother yet. Love from Norman. P.S. And love from Mum, Dad, Belinda, Joan, Winnie and Mary Frances. XOXOXOXOXOX.' Even when she went out, Vera carried it in her pocket.

Christmas week and a long-standing acquaintance arrived in town and gave her a call. She went to the hotel. His friend, the senator, was with him and she had a bad time. She had a lot to drink – had to have a lot to drink. On her way out of the hotel, she bought stamps in the lobby, put nine fifty-dollar bills into an envelope, no note, and mailed them to Norman. She considered stopping off somewhere on her way home across town but what was the point? She stopped only to buy a bottle, then continued on her way to 10th Avenue.

'There's gotta be something better than this.' A line from a song that she laughed at; friends in the business called it to one another when things were bad. Now, stilled, her lips moved silently over the words.

Dear Mom. She should write to her family. Dear, dear Mom. My dearest grandmother, how are you? Dearest, dearest, dearest Mom. Last time she was home she should have made time to visit Mom instead of that stupid poxy lunch. She should not say things like that about her family. Dear Tom. Tom always frightened her a little. Frightened her. Flaming. But that was because they were for your good, brothers. Dear Tom. And dear Caitriona, and dear Martina, and dear Joe, and dear – Oh, Christ! What was the other one's name? Dear Norman, how beautiful your card is and do you know how much it means to me? Fuck! Dear Norman, Marcia – Wrong way round. Dear Marcia, Henry, Norman, Belinda, Winnie, Joan, Mary Frances, Tom, Caitriona, Martina, Joe, Aisling, Mary Jane, Declan. Dear Mom – Dear Mom – Dear Mom – Dear Mom – Dear Mom!

'Yes, it would be a good idea, Baby Vera,' she told herself out loud, rising, 'to have something to write with if you are going to write,' and fell back into her chair. 'Well, I never,' she said, 'drunk and fucked silly!' Another effort: 'But Baby Vera is a survivor – see!' and got up this time to search for a biro. 'Baby Vera is talking to herself and why not, for God's sake, I ask you, why-fucking-not! Nckdwicminthorld!'

On a shelf in the kitchen, behind the coffee and the sugar and the cookies – 'I ask you, fucking cookies!' – was a brown jar with its lid taped down – 'In case of accidental use!' – containing the ashes of her boyfriend, Wally the Swede. What was a big whore like her to do with ashes? Was there a point in keeping ashes, looking at ashes, taking them down? 'No!' No need to shout. Is there any affection to be derived from fucking ashes? 'No. Simply. No.' What was she to do with Wally the Swede?

Aaw, is Baby Vera crying?

You're no good, Vera, you never were, you do not belong. All you were ever good for was a good time.

'Good time, did you say a good time? Shit? – Actual shit! – Eat it?' Fucking animals. 'No!' Fucking animals do not stoop so low. Or if they do they have a purpose. Nature gives animals a purpose if they behave like that, but not human beings.

'Yeah-yeah-yeah, but you're no good, you just do not belong, so there, so what are you going to do about it?' Now is your chance.

Will you? Won't you? 'Yes?' You have the wherewithal. 'No?' So that has taken care of that one. I thought that that would be your answer.

Good fucking time, I ask you. Fucking animals, fucking shit, fucking senators, fucking hotels and hotel fucking rooms, who're yeh kidding, fucking whore, for fuck's sake, fucking hotel, fucking family.

The bottle nearly drunk, with variations on the message, but basically saying the same thing, she wrote on three Christmas cards: I'm no fucking good. Make me a fucking offer. Love, Vera. And mailed them in the dawn to Tom, Marcia and Mary Jane. She did not hear from them again for several months.

The only communication in the meantime was a beer-stained card that arrived in late January or early February. It cheered her up; she thought he had forgotten. 'Dear Vera, a bilated Happy Xmas and a Bright New Year from your old beau Finbar.'

She was approaching the outskirts of the town now. B-&-B signs swung unproductively outside houses that were thriftily refusing to acknowledge with any form of light that night had all but established itself. Where to stay was the question. She hadn't thought about it until now. The hotel was closed down. She did not want to stay with Tom, Marcia or Mary Jane. Oh, for various reasons. They didn't know she was coming: that was one good reason. Really, she didn't want to see them at all.

'Grange', said the sign, the name of the town, and, under it, 'Fáilte', welcome. And she began to feel nervous. What was it she had come home for?

Impulsively, she took the next left, leaving the main road that would have brought her to the town centre, and drove through the New Estate. The New Estate was built just about the time she was born. Terraces of grim semi-detached houses, the front gardens, almost every one, looking like scrapyards. A piebald pony wandered aimlessly past battered-looking Ford cars and Hiace vans, broken glass and debris littered the street, children shrugged in casual defiance out of the way, refusing to be impressed by a silver Merc, a dog was barking across the street at a man out walking greyhounds. Though it was a small town by standards, six or seven thousand people, she knew very little about this quarter other than had she taken the next left – or was it the one after that? – off the main road back there, she would have been pretty close to where Finbar Reilly lived.

She found her way out of the New Estate and into a newer one. But her sense of direction was good. She was by-passing the town, looking for the country on the other side of it. Unconsciously, she was making for Mom's. 'PS. Mom dead.'

Tom's letter, unlike his previous ones, was typewritten and 'Department of Industry and Commerce' on the government note-paper that he always used was scissored off.

Bellevue Heights,
Cnoc Mhuire,
Grange.

May 15th 1974

Dear Vera,

I am writing to inform you that Miss M. Rooney has left the hotel. As reasons for her resignation she supplied the following: a) That she could no longer continue as manageress of an establishment supposedly owned by an absentee. b) That she could no longer continue to accept advice which she considered to be interference from any party connected with the O'Toole name. Her manner to me personally was offensive in the extreme and I have discovered since that she behaved in a likewise manner to your sister Mrs. Mary Jane Mansfield. Her conduct was atrocious and if you do not understand me having no option but to accept her resignation on the spot then that is too bad, Vera. She then demanded a month's back-pay and three weeks' holiday money. It being a matter of honour I gave her my own personal cheque for the total amount and requested a receipt which she gave me.

I then had a lengthy meeting with your sister Mrs. Mary Jane Mansfield to discuss what should be done. We should be failing in our duty if we did not say the following: Why – can you supply a straight answer? – should I put my wife in there when she has enough to do at home? Why allow her to tend services without maybe as much as a thank you in the end? Why should I continue to jeopardize my job trying to look after your affairs? You seem to forget that I have a responsible Government job to look after as well as my role of a father attempting to bring up three children in a proper manner. And why should your sister Mrs. Mary Jane Mansfield out of the goodness of her heart continue either to worry about your welfare and spend sleepless nights? A fella would be very interested to hear the answers to them ones.

There being no other way I then, together with your sister Mrs. Mary Jane Mansfield, we went to the hotel on the following night to speak to and negotiate with the remaining staff. After negotiations too lengthy to go into here they have been paid off and each given one week's wages in lieu of holidays and the hotel has been closed as of and including February 24th. All accounts, receipts and relevant materials have been deposited with Mr. Tommy Martin, Solrs., High Street, Grange.

Forthrightly I do not know what you think you are playing at but your sisters and I would also like to ask have you forgotten what it is like to live in a small town and the pride we take in it. New York indeed and I am sure is New York but a name means something here. We have a sense of place. We have a sense of responsibility. We aspire to become moral agents without apology to anyone because that is our greatest desire, Vera. The same as our mother and father, I think we here have an idea of the direction of the right road to ethics.

I would never say we are 100% flawless nor maybe even near that figure but give full marks, 100% for effort. If I sound like I am boasting, without demur put my name down first under the word boast on that score. Your choice of life is your own business but do not try to insist on your choice on us. Leave that to us, Vera. We know what is right.

I had not intended to raise the subject of your communication that came in the letter-box of my home over Christmas and the letter-boxes of your sisters. You can hardly have considered that it was funny to introduce such matter into the abodes of innocence where children reside. We sincerely hope that there shall not be a repeat. Further, all I can say is that you left us hurt, astonished at what you wrote on Christmas cards and, frankly, baffled as to your motives.

Therefore I have as of yesterday sought legal advice in the presence of your sister Mrs. Mary Jane Mansfield. (In case you should be interested in your other sister, Mrs. Marcia Locke-Browne is due any minute now.) The advice we received is that the Imperial Hotel be put on the market for you. That the sale be not by Private Treaty, be not by any private or confidential method of conveyancing, but be by Public Auction. Public Auction being the public way and the fair way. That is the legal advice coming to you free of charge. And that is also the advice coming to you from your brother and sisters. If you agree – and we sincerely hope that you do – the advice then is: a) For fair play, that you do not deal with any member of your family, i.e., Thomas O'Toole, Mrs. Mary Jane Mansfield, Mrs. Marcia Locke-Browne. b) That you deal solely and direct with Mr. Tommy Martin, Solrs., High Street, Grange. All you have to write is: Dear Mr. Martin, I should be obliged if you would put The Imperial Hotel, The Square, Grange, up for sale by public auction on my behalf. And sign your name. He will then engage an auctioneer, etc. You do not have to come home for it. But it will all be done in the open.

Finally, I am not a man for shutting doors and let me state that, after the auction, my door and the doors of your sisters' homes will always remain open as always. I hope that this finds you in good health. And so, on my own behalf and on the behalfs of your sisters, fond regards and God bless.

Your affectionate brother,

Tom.

PS. Mom dead.

IV

THE GRANDMOTHER

Hard to imagine that life existed in that house. But it did. Several generations, a hundred and fifty years of life. People not given much to smiling but when they did children's eyes responded, their hearts leaped for joy as in a great mystery just explained.

Hard to imagine that as recently as . . . When did she die? When did the little sounds stop that you could hear from the room? The tongs in the morning grubbing in the ashes, the kettle being filled, being put on the hook, the water thrown out, falling like a carpet on the yard, clank of the lid on the iron pot, eagerness of the knife sawing through bread, tongs in the fire again last thing at night, raking over the ashes. When did they stop? How did she die?

Sheep and lambs brushed each side of the car, the same she had passed back there on the road; the man in the wellingtons following, his hands in a flap, exasperated as before with his fitful flock; the young black and white dog, now chastened, following in silent disgrace. The man turning back once more to warn the dog before calling ahead to the distance, to someone out of sight to come out and guard the road, turn the sheep into a field.

The stars were out, there was a bright May moon, there was a white frost. The indifference of the house. The thatch was heavy, dead, the windows flat, as if made of some black material, the door sealed, dumb, as if she had bolted it from inside, then rolled up stones against it to harden it, so that none could enter; the tomb secured, had then undressed in the kitchen and washed herself; the habit from the brown parcel and dressed in it; the surprise of hair unloosed from the bun and brushed it; then gone to the room, lit candles and laid herself down on top of the bedspread, wanting none to sit around her but to decree that life in that little house had to, must, cease with her.

Vera felt friendless. She had arrived half an hour ago and pulled up, half on the road, half on the apron of grass that sloped down from the road to the house. She had not got out. What point getting out?

'D'you know, you're the best girl in the world.' 'Stay there, child, it's too cold to get up.' 'The sun shines bright on my old Kentucky home, 'tis summer, the darkies are gay.' 'I won't forget you, Vera.'

And, as best Vera could remember it, there had been a period of aloofness at the start, as if Mom was being cautious of her. But it did not last long, and Vera was brought from the other room – 'It's damp!' – to Mom's room, to share the big bed.

'Stay there, child, it's too cold to go to school.' And she would return with mugs of tea and her own bread and they'd stay on there together. You could feel the warmth rising from her great body. 'You'll be as big as myself, Vera, on my oath you will, the size of the feet on you!' The brass knob that unscrewed off the post at the foot of the bed that you could hide secrets in. And they'd lie on there, contentedly silent after the breakfast, or reciting sums, or poems, or singing, until it was time by mutual consent – Vera was always consulted – for them to get up and put on the dinner for the two of them.

'I won't forget you, Vera' was what she said the day Vera's mother came out for Vera. Cross words were spoken; her mother lost control. Vera watched secretly from the room but could not quite understand the mystery. Something about Uncle Willie who had come back from San Jose and Mom had taken him in and Vera's mother had heard.

'Is this place going to be mine or not?'

'We'll see,' said Mom, 'I'm not dead yet.'

Something about Uncle Willie not being a full uncle.

'The child is somewhere,' said Mom in a growl, 'keep your voice down.'

'Is he the fiddler's, the thatcher's, the tinker's son, maybe?'

'I'm no less his mother than yours,' said Mom.

Vera's mother's face growing bigger and nearly in on top of Mom's: 'A thing from a ditch, a thing from a ditch!'

Mom's face darkening, but bowing solemnly, yes.

'Vera is coming home!'

Mom bowed, too, to this, the same grave way.

Her mother then, beginning to look beaten, was turning away, as if to start crying, but Vera held her breath because she knew there was more to come. And she was right. Didn't her mother come wheeling back in a flurry of temper and clawing at Mom's front.

'Stop!' The heel of Mom's fist sounded hollowly on her mother's chest.

Vera came in at this stage to smile at them.

'Stop,' said Mom again, this time to herself, and sat down on the box by the hearth.

And Uncle Willie only outside in an outhouse, only looking at his glass eye in the mirror!

But it was over now. Her mother's quick movements, heels clicking the concrete floor, to and fro with the bag, packing Vera's things. Mom's straight back by the hearth, neck craned, her back to them, her hands composed. She had a dignity that few knew about or even suspected, which was a pity. But she was deeply upset. And when Vera's mother went out with the bag, 'I'm going now,' said Vera.

Mom nodded in the slow formal manner but she did not turn her head or stand up.

Maybe she had not heard properly and Vera went and stood beside her, 'Mom?' for a kiss. 'I'm going now.'

'I won't forget you, Vera,' she said and twisted her face away to look up at the ceiling.

Of course, later on, Vera understood what it was all about. The farm, and getting pregnant. That her grandmother had got pregnant out of wedlock, in well-established widowhood, that Uncle Willie was only a half-brother to her mother and that her mother was frightened for the farm.

The young black and white dog that she had seen earlier was approaching, turning circles on the road, running backwards to someone who was following and forwards again. The earlier humiliation with the sheep was forgotten, he frisked about the car and inspected the apron of grass in front of the house and then continued on. An elderly woman, stooped, was following and she too passed by without looking, her head thrust forward in front of a rigidly inclined body. After a few yards she returned.

'Is it Vera?'

Mrs Conneeley from a quarter of a mile up the road. Conneeley's house and Mom's were the only two on this stretch of road. She too was a widow: Mom had laid out her husband. She had two small children, boys, when Vera used to visit her as a child. Vera let the window slide down on the passenger side.

'Is it Vera? D'you know we were saying it might be you? Aw, is it Vera! Paddy was out with the sheep and said maybe it was you so I came over just in case. How are you, how are you!'

Vera got out and Mrs Conneeley embraced her, then took her hands and held on to them tightly.

'Poor Mom, the creature,' she said. 'I wish we were meeting under different circumstances. But d'you know I'm so pleased to see you.' Her eyes were bright as a bird's. 'You'll come over for a cup of tea. You will, you will, you will, you will, you will!'

Vera laughed – the sound of her own laughter surprising her – responding to the warmth, and she was happy to be unable to refuse the invitation.

'I'll be there before you,' said Mrs Conneeley, refusing any idea of a lift, and already set off homeward along the road, her arm like a wing repeatedly flapping, waving Vera to follow in the car.

Conneeley's old house was still standing. It, too, was white-washed, thatched and closed up, like Mom's. A section of the loose stone wall that fronted the next field was gone and was replaced by a wall in coloured stone with ornamental railings on top. There were concrete paths: the wide one, muddied, leading to a yard from where sheep could be heard bleating, the narrower one to the front door, bisecting a lawn of sorts. The house was also built in coloured stone, a bungalow, and had picture windows. It was very warm inside and children's clothes were airing on the rail of a Raeburn cooker.

Mrs Conneeley had been dissuaded from putting down a fire in the front room. They had been living in the new house since 1967 but she still missed an open fire in the kitchen.

'But if you open the door to the grate on that gazebo you at least have a place to spit.'

She laughed happily and busied herself, removing the children's clothes and making the tea. Paddy nodded to Vera behind his mother's back and winked at his mother's excitement. He introduced his wife to Vera. They had four children, all under the age of eight. They were going up to make the last hour in Melody's for a few drinks. The young dog, Starsky, had no sense and was called in before Paddy left with his wife, lest he should follow the car.

Francis, the other son, was married in England and ran a pub there. He was talking about coming home. The old house was his and the field behind it. If you left the roof on the old house you stood a better chance of getting building permission for another new one, or at least that's what they said. That's why they hadn't knocked it down.

'Well, I'm so pleased to see you,' said Mrs Conneeley again. 'Pull down to the fire,' she said, blowing her nose.

They sat around the Raeburn, the door of it open so that they could see the turf burning inside it. 'It makes great bread, though,' said Mrs Conneeley appreciatively, and she smiled to herself. 'Lord, she was a powerful, strong woman in her time,' she said then. 'Mighty. And not much loss in her, mind you, towards the end. The sight was what troubled her most. Oh now, when the sight begins to go, Vera. And you're not unlike her, God bless you. I can see the resemblance.'

'What age did they put on the coffin?' said Vera.

'We were talking about that all right,' said Mrs Conneeley. 'Eighty-six?'

Vera considered this. 'Yes, that would be right,' she said. 'She told me she was born – ' Vera laughed ' – about a dozen years before the century, she said. And was married in nineteen-hundred and five, aged about seventeen.'

'That'd be about right, then,' said Mrs Conneeley. 'Eighty-six.' And she was pleased, as was Vera, that no error had been made on the breastplate. Then she frowned at the cooker in a new thought. 'And sure you must be – ' She searched Vera's face. 'Thirty-four?'

'The last time I saw thirty-four, Mrs Conneeley,' said Vera, 'was on top of a bus.'

And they burst out laughing at age, Mrs Conneeley's head bobbing over her rigid spine until, remembering her sleeping grandchildren, she put a finger to her lips.

'I'll be thirty-eight this week,' said Vera, and laughed again. She felt drunk in this warmth of friendship. She could not stop smiling.

'And what age am I?' said Mrs Conneeley. 'Try a guess.'

Vera would have thought late seventies or thereabouts. Maybe more. She saw Mrs Conneeley as belonging to Mom's generation. The thin hair, the bright, bird-like eyes. She considered the distorted frame, the age that had passed since the woman sitting opposite her had been widowed.

'I haven't a clue,' she said.

Mrs Conneeley was sixty-four, her mother's generation, not Mom's. But, of course, when you considered that she had to bring up two children and work the farm on her own. And those buckets! Vera remembered that she always appeared to be carrying two buckets, the buckets hanging down from her, clear of the slant of her body.

'Sixty-four,' said Mrs Conneeley again, proudly.

And Vera was glad to be sharing Mrs Conneeley's pride and to be included so naturally in this household where laughter and conversation came so easily.

She thought about Mom again. She had always thought of Mom as an old woman but now she calculated that Mom was still comparatively young when she went to live with her.

'I saw some nice cattle in Mom's front field as I was driving over,' said Vera, wanting the conversation to keep going. 'Whose are they at all, at all?'

'Your brother's,' said Mrs Conneeley sitting up straight as she could for a moment. 'He has it stocked these two months,' she said, and waited.

'When did she die?' said Vera and immediately felt a collapse within herself. She who had lived with Mom, felt secret pride in being told that she resembled her, did not know the date of her grandmother's death.

Mrs Conneeley did not appear to notice Vera's shame. 'The last week in February,' she said. 'It's a terrible month for death.'

February. Vera had thought this month, May, or maybe the end of April. Why hadn't they written or cabled her? Those stupid Christmas cards, was it?

But now something further was going badly wrong. Mrs Conneeley's bird-like eyes were watering over, becoming opaque, and she was smiling painfully at Vera. 'And sure she'd have lasted another ten years,' she said.

The smile closing on Vera's face.

'Aw, God, Vera,' she said.

Vera holding her breath.

'Sure she'd have lasted another ten years if someone got to her.'

Mrs Conneeley could see the waiting alarm but she could not stop now. She was looking at Vera helplessly, for understanding, for permission to continue.

'I'd be ashamed,' she said, 'if people were to think us bad neighbours.'

Vera nodded, which was the last thing she wanted to do.

'She was very strong, d'you know. But I knew for a long time the sight was going. You'd know it the way she wouldn't recognize you sometimes until you spoke. And I started to go over to see her, d'you know, and tell Paddy, any time he was passing to call in, or I'd bring her over the drop of soup or whatever was in the saucepan. That way. Because, though she was that kind of private class of woman, independent, she was good, and was first to your aid if you needed it. And I know well about that. And Paddy'd go over to give her the riding to Mass of a Sunday and home again – or at least he'd ask, because sometimes she liked the walk. Or to take her to the village for the pension of a Friday, and the few groceries. But your brother didn't like it. Oh, I don't know. Maybe, I suppose, he thought we were after the farm. It happens.'

Her voice was soft, without hope, as if she knew she was praying to an insensible God. Then her spine craning backwards to bring her head up, attempting pride, her face trying to twist itself out of its misery. Her eyes had become fierce and they fastened on Vera, as if Vera were a stranger, or a familiar adversary.

'But how much land does anyone need?' she said. 'I know how much land a person needs. And mine know it. How much land does Mom Lally need now? How much does the man who used to be my husband need? Or anyone else that's living or dead, for that matter?'

The defiance was a momentary thing and, as if it hadn't happened, as if she had spoken unaware of herself, her body shrank forward again to continue to the fire.

'But your brother came out one evening and Paddy was in with her. And your brother followed Paddy out as he was leaving to come home. And he said to Paddy that he was sure Paddy had more to be doing without visiting old women, and tell your mother the same, he said. What could we do? Paddy was shaking telling me. What could we do?'

Mrs Conneeley inhaled deeply, then tried to let her breath out silently. A child cried in its sleep for a moment from one of the rooms.

'Poor Mom,' said Mrs Conneeley to herself and threw a few sods of turf into the grate and watched the sparks.

Vera waited, a half-smile transfixing her face. Mrs Conneeley smiled painfully again at her. Vera nodded.

'I think it was a Wednesday and Paddy came in. Julia was there, feeding the youngest. I don't see any smoke he said coming from Mom Lally's, did you see her at all since Sunday? We left Julia there and went over the two of us, first, to pass by, then look in the windows. But it was hard to see in. And I called out her name, d'you know. And Paddy tried the door but it was bolted. I don't care, he said then, and I nodded to him to go ahead.'

She began to weep, her whole face moving, looking from the fire to Vera and back again, not knowing where to put her eyes. Vera, now, nodding vigorous encouragement.

'Oh, she was dead, Vera. Oh, she was dead. Oh, Vera.'

Mrs Conneeley trying to swallow; Vera waiting for her to continue.

'She'd fell. She was there for a few days, d'you know. She'd fell into the fire. But she got out of it. She'd got out of it some way, the creature, crawled. But couldn't get up. What could we do? It isn't like us to be bad neighbours. No one wants to be like that.'

She was weeping bitterly, leaning forward in her chair, one hand covering her face, the other held out and back to Vera. Vera took the hand and held it almost absently. She was sitting bolt upright and tears were running down her face. She frowned, shook her head in denial. But it would not go away. There was something terribly wrong. Not poxy, fucking Christmas cards. There was something terribly wrong.

Mrs Conneeley came out to see her off and they shook hands.

'You're staying in the hotel.'

'Yes.'

She stopped the car again for a moment outside Mom's. It would have been disrespectful – irreverent – just to have driven past. Oh Jesus, what prayer did one say in such desolation?

But she, herself, too, had let Mom down. Did she really, so easily, accept that Tom would look after Mom? Tom? Who was Tom? But wasn't she, herself, simple, stupid, lazy, selfish? Yes.

As a child, when she returned to live in the town, and heard it whispered, 'She hasn't the morals of a dog,' she prayed Hail Marys for Mom's soul. Did they say that about Mom because she was a widow-woman who got drunk once a week, or because she had an illegitimate child, or because she wouldn't put a name on a piece of paper for them? And Vera had worked it out in Conneeley's that night, that if Mom was born about a dozen years before the century, married when she was seventeen in 1905, widowed in 1910, buried Uncle Willie in his thirty-sixth year in 1951, she must have had her illegitimate child, Uncle Willie, fathered by thatcher, tinker or fiddler in 1915: then Mom, her grandmother, the widow-woman, was twenty-seven years of age at the time.

The sign in the headlights on this side of town also said 'Grange', the name of the town, and 'Fáilte', welcome. Of course she wasn't staying in the fucking hotel: late as it was, tired as she was, she wanted to get out of it, get back to Dublin, the plane, get away.

She took the detour again to by-pass the town, drove through the yellow-brick estate and into the one with glass on the street. A man walking homeward with the hunched-up shoulders of a drunk, a group of youths hanging over railings in some kind of wrestling that looked more dangerous than the real thing, televisions sporadically lighting up windows: it was all but deserted.

Then she saw the piebald pony. He was standing, head hung, like a tired sentry, dead centre at the top of the street where she would have to turn right for Dublin. She slowed down, flashed her lights, but he continued immobile, his eyes screwed upwards, fixed on her in the lights. She came to a halt. The weariness on the pony's face was as hers. She had a bottle in her bag. She was tired. She didn't care. She drove the Merc on to the footpath to the left of the pony and turned left into the main road, back towards the town. The railway bridge was up ahead. She turned left again before the bridge and into a deserted street of railway houses. One of the streets off this one would take her back into another part of the New Estate. She found it and then found number 17. Maybe he would let her in.

V

FIRST LOVE

'Just a, just a, just a!' He affected a bout of coughing to avoid making a statement and to cover his alarm. 'Just a minute!'

He hurried back to the room to cover himself, pull on his trousers, and his shoes in case he had to stand on the cold doorstep. Can I come in, was that what she said? The fucking empty beer cans and Guinness bottles about the bed. He picked a plate up off the floor and threw its greasy contents, the remnants of a meal, into the fire. The fucking spoon and knife followed. Where to put the plate? Ceremoniously he put the plate on the bed, told himself there was no panic, then returned along the hall, brushing the wall with the back of his hand and coughing politely.

'Hello dare, Swannee River!' he said.

'Hi!' said Vera apologetically. 'Can I come in?'

'Jesus, Mary and Joseph, you put the heart crossways in me!'

He had already registered the overnight bag and, more alarmingly, over her shoulder, the silver Merc under the street-lamp outside his gate. There was no way out of it.

'Liberty Hall, as the fella said!' he said, stepping outside so that she could enter. 'Watch your step.'

Vera went in.

The light from the street-lamp carried only a little way into the hall, then her bag caught on something and a tangle of bentwood chairs collapsed on the floor behind her. Other objects of furniture and bric-à-brac shifted and made warning noises on the stairs above her. She laughed softly and continued along the narrow path, keeping close to the wall that was free of stacked-up furniture.

Finbar felt sudden resentment of her laugh. That freedom of personality!

'The lights are gone,' he said to himself. Then he came in and closed the door. He stepped over the chairs and followed to the candle-lit room.

'Well!' he said. 'This is a surprise! What? This is – how shall I put it? – a total surprise! Sit down. And it was only the – Sit on this one, the fucking springs are broke on that.'

There was a stack of old newspapers and he took the top one and threw it on to the seat of the good chair.

'Excuse the French,' he said. 'Dog hairs. And it was only the other day I was thinking about you. You're welcome, sit down, you're welcome.'

He straightened himself and his head and shoulders became lost in the comparative darkness above the flickering light of the candle. He spread his hands over the visible chaos of the room.

'I'm afraid it's the maid's day off,' he said. 'What? What?'

'Would you like a drink?' she said.

He took a flashlamp from the mantelpiece and went out to the adjoining room, a back-kitchen, where she heard him running water. He was washing something.

She unbuttoned her coat.

The smell of stale beer and cigarettes was familiar, of course; and the acridity: that came from the bed, more than likely; there was a smell of grease, mutton. The smell of dogs, so pervasive, was new to her but not at all off-putting. On the contrary. She could distinguish too – it reminded her of somewhere – the smell of raw eggs; and the smell of damp, or was it dried-out wallpaper?

She unzipped her bag, produced a bottle of Wild Turkey and placed it on the floor in front of her.

A mound of ashes grew out of the grate, covering the hearth-stone, almost to her feet: silver paper and half-burnt cigarette packets jutted out here and there and, yes, there were eggshells half-buried in the ashes. Something was fizzing in the embers and issuing jets of smoke, adding another taste to the room. No, not at all off-putting. The room had a character that could keep the world at bay.

She undid the clasp at the top of her blouse and the lapels fell away from her throat. She pocketed the clasp and then considered the next button down. Not yet.

He returned with two wet glasses.

'Well! Well! What's new?' he said. 'What? – When did you arrive? – Did you feel the touch of frost out there? – "Speak your word, said the guard at the gate, yes but bear it to Caesar straight!" – When did you arrive?'

'Just now,' she said.

He placed the glasses on the floor and she poured the drinks with great concentration. Then she looked up at him admiringly.

'Down the hatch!'

'Jesus, that's lovely,' he said. 'What is it?'

He sat on the stack of newspapers and started to break kindling with his hands, an orange box; then he took a newspaper from under him and twisted the pages into bows which, together with the kindling, he placed on the embers and, on top of these, heavier pieces of polished timber, the broken legs of an antique.

'Humphrey Bogart,' he said. 'Bourbon, my first ever taste of it.'

43

A brilliant fire.

During its blossoming and withering his chattering continued, reciting snippets of poetry and telling her stories. But he was beginning to relax and, before repeating the ritual of the fire, he grubbed in the ashes – 'Hey presto cockolorum!' – and produced items of cutlery on the end of the tongs. His body rocked and swayed on his stool of newspapers, his head almost touching her knees. And she laughed back gratefully, and at the glaze of whiskey that was appearing and the shine of daring.

'Can I stay?'

He stood up, waved his hands, flapped them to his sides. 'You're here!' he said and sat down. Then up again to qualify what he had just said, inform her in grand gestures that the house, effectively, in extent, was what she saw before her: the room that they were sitting in, the back-kitchen off it and something more vague beyond the back-kitchen.

She understood the terms.

'Can I stay for a few days?'

He sat again, something bothering him about this. 'What about the fucking car?' he said in a whisper. And then explained: 'The Punjab.'

She understood. If it was going to be a matter of a few days, the car, a Merc, could not be left parked on a street in the New Estate.

He was pulling on a jersey. 'Give me the keys,' he said.

'Can you drive?'

'A-a-w!' She had offended him. 'Is it an aeroplane then?'

She gave him the keys. 'Leave it until morning,' she said.

'I'll do it now,' he said reflectively, 'while I'm drunk.'

She laughed at him and then he laughed at himself. The muffled laughter of conspirators.

'No, it's better to do it now while it's dark. Though I know someone will fucking spot me. This town!' He had his jacket on and was searching among the bedclothes for an overcoat. 'But

44

where'll I park it, what? Maybe the most obvious place, nobody knows it's yours.'

'Not on the Square.'

'I'll think of something,' he said. 'Yeh.'

'I'll stay here so.'

He was paused, reflecting his route, his course of action.

'Yeh.' And before leaving, he said, 'In case you're interested, that's a candle, and or, that's a flashlamp, and my place of ablutions is out there through a door in the back-kitchen.'

She heard him step over the chairs in the hall and the door closing behind him.

The bed was small, a single bed. Should she be on the outside or the inside? The outside, she decided: he was the smaller body. The back of one of the armchairs pulled up against the bed before falling asleep would stop her falling out on to the floor. She would have to stay awake until he returned; it was only fair. She was tired and if you touched her on the shoulder she would keel over, but she wasn't drunk or sleepy: that kind of tiredness. So, it was an ill wind that didn't blow somebody good. And by the same process of thinking, though she could not be whole-hearted about anything in her present state of mind, an occasion had arisen for her long-standing curiosity about him. So, it was an ill wind that didn't, etc.

How many clothes to take off? She had already taken off her coat and fingered down the buttons of her blouse and it hung open. She unzipped her suede skirt and stepped out of it. Better not, as yet, produce slippers; better not at all. Leave the knickers and bra on. She did not want to frighten him. She knew from experience that it would take two or three days to recover from the cloud that had descended and she needed the claustrophobia of this room to hole up in. Then she would go back.

The lavatory was located in a section off the back-kitchen; the cistern, up near the ceiling, wept or leaked moisture; the place of ablutions was a single tap that hung wonkily over a heavy earthenware sink in front of a window in the back-kitchen. Finbar's things and his mirror were on the sash.

After washing, she returned to the room and got into the bed to wait. Shadows, like fish, darted across the ceiling, then grew ragged wings, became birds, exploded and were sucked down into a dark wood. She tested the reaching distance from the bed to the leg of the armchair. It was satisfactorily positioned for the moment. When fishes flew and forests walked.

The short-cut to the schools was through the park and she used to watch from the shadows under the trees. The air under the trees was less pure but more exciting: you could smell it coming up out of the ground. She used to kneel there. The idea of a smiling devil was clever but one as young as ten-and-a-half? It took an unusual hold of her imagination the year that she returned from the country, and she used to go into the shadows beneath the trees and kneel as if to tie a shoe-lace or as if to order the books in her satchel but, really, to watch the faces of unsuspecting schoolboys passing by from the CBS, the primary school. She couldn't see it.

There was a boy, though, who did not appear to go to school at all, who hung about the park or on street corners, waiting for chums to be let out, and to influence them, it was said. Finbar Reilly was much older than the Redemptorist's ten-and-a-half and by no means was he a smiler. Very much the opposite, in fact. He even whistled and played the Jew's-harp with a frown, threw stones at his faithful dog who, despite all, continued a decent, smiling sort. He was clearly more interested in eating beechnuts and thinking about himself than in morality. But wasn't that it! The devil was clever in his disguises and had more than one trick up his sleeve. And, now, when Vera saw Finbar approaching in the street, she held her head a little higher, breathed through her nose, tried not to breathe at all when abreast of him and, in the second of just having passed him by, gave an extra swish to her ponytail. Or if she saw him up ahead of her in the park, she lengthened her stride and passed him out, fortified in the Miraculous Medal in her fist. Though she saw him somewhere almost every schoolday, his dark preoccupation with himself continued, so much so that she was beginning to think that maybe she was mistaken about him, that he was, maybe, nothing at all.

Then, one day, he wasn't there any more; he just disappeared; and it was as if no one but herself noticed the fact. And he was gone for a whole year and a half.

She got an awful start at the Sunday matinée. The younger children were in the stalls, shrieking at the film. She was in the balcony with her friends and, as was the custom, they were turning back now and again to hand sweets or throw them, and nuts, to the boys in the rows behind them. Then, later, sweet-papers and nut-shells would be thrown forward by the boys on to the girls' hair: a kind of ritual. Suddenly she became aware of a presence behind her. Sniggering, rustling, creaking came from everywhere else but, two rows behind her, there was someone in a pocket of silence and chills ran up and down her spine. She hadn't noticed him come in; she hadn't even known that he was back; it was as if he had materialized in the dark out of thin air.

Then, of course, the usual, old, next phase in the ritual. Sweets and sweet-papers, nuts and nut-shells exhausted, the bombardment done, the boys were coming forward, climbing over the backs of seats for engagements with the girls of a closer kind. Indeed, one of them landed on the seat right next to her – she knew him and his disgusting tricks – and any time she adjusted herself in her seat to talk to the girl on the other side of her, his hand, palm down, would attempt to slide in under her, until she simply changed her place entirely, left the row she was in and took an aisle seat further back, in the row behind the one that Finbar was sitting in.

Outside in the sunshine, the film over, she stood in her circle of girlfriends. The boys were now as good as pie, of course, keeping to their own company. Then a circle of them gathered to trap a tin can and started kicking one another's shins, worse than children, and obscuring her view. They broke and now she could observe

47

Finbar again at the cinema wall. He was still a frowner and she watched him shrug dubiously about something to the boys who were with him. She didn't care, she wanted to catch his eye. And when she did, she nodded her sober acknowledgement of his return. He showed little or no reaction but as she went home, immediately and alone, she discovered an extraordinary secret happiness growing within her.

An involuntary muscular movement, she felt her knees press together, her thighs tighten on her forearm. She withdrew her arm and then took her hand upwards to stroke the curve of her belly, then downwards again, through the hair, turned the fingers in between her legs to find the it of the girl, the what, the quem, gee, the job, the word that offended her, the font, the nothing, the everything, the hole, to find it wet. Good. When fishes flew and forests walked and whatever the rest of it is.

It was innocent first love.

There was so much resistance in reaction to their first meeting that the affair became inevitable. They began, as it was called, to do a line. It began in September and ended early in the following January. Now he was sixteen. They didn't have much conversation but this was compensated for by his playing the mouth-organ – if not well, then in a determined way – and he gave her tries, as they walked the two miles to the dairy and the river and back again. He told her that he was practising, that he was going to join a band and that he would progress to the saxophone by watching regularly and at close quarters how they did it. But they were mostly silent, whether walking side by side, standing or sitting on a wall. They smoked cigarettes and wiped their noses secretly when they felt a kiss was coming on. Whatever about Finbar, Vera kept precious count in a diary. Two, four, six, five and, on a wet Sunday afternoon, under the trees in Woodlawn, nine, when she was meant to be rehearsing *Romeo and Juliet* in the convent.

She knew now that he had been lifted, just like that, by the authorities, had been made to vanish for a whole year and a half.

One night she asked him, 'Where were you?'

His look, startled at first, became furtive, then blank when he remembered who she was; his mouth moved to smile but was unable to complete it because of a memory already become ageless. He shook his head and looked away, pursing his lips in a silent whistle.

'Where?' she asked again, innocently.

'Nickerdepazze,' he said quietly, blowing his tuneless whistle again at the dark in front of him, the nightmare of the Industrial School that he could not share where there was a graveyard with one hundred children.

The town had the news of Finbar Reilly's and Vera O'Toole's line and of Vera's family being scandalized. After study, eight o'clock, her father would be waiting outside the convent gates. He would simply nod to her and mouth the word, 'Home', and then would follow a few paces behind her. When her mother upbraided her, sometimes beat her and pulled her hair, if her father was present, he would stand there, pierced, with a look of powerful distaste on his face for Vera, like someone who had just witnessed a bad accident.

Finbar was lower than a tinker.

Vera, during those months, was fortunate only in that Finbar's mother was not known to have or have had TB: her friend, Sally Downey, was beaten regularly, not only by her parents but also by her brothers.

Still, she and Finbar persisted.

The Parish Priest was called in. He interviewed them separately, Finbar in the presbytery, Vera in the hotel. She met the Superintendent of the Garda, in uniform, going up the stairs of the hotel one morning as she was coming down to go to school. Maybe there was no connection, but she had her suspicions because he didn't say a word to her. A nun told her to stay on one evening after school, then a second one came in with a bottle and sprinkled holy water on her. The holy water was the worst of all and it

49

worried her, but when she joined her friends who were waiting in the convent grounds to hear what had happened, Vera laughed and said, 'Shite on them!' Tom got the flu and though Vera knew she was perfectly well, the doctor examined her too.

She saved up all her money and, together with a postal order, a Christmas present, used it to buy an electric razor for Finbar. They met in the lane that the yards of the shops in High Street backed on to. She presented it to him in the dark. She didn't want anything in return. She saw the glint of the mouth-organ down at his side and she knew that he was seriously considering giving it to her. She hooped her arms loosely over his shoulders, she only wanted to be his girlfriend. She slid the hoop of her arms down his body and tightened it, to pin his arms so that he should keep the mouth-organ. She only wanted him not to weaken.

A figure, a Garda, came out of the pub yard opposite to where they were standing and staggered into the darkness beside them. She felt the hand fall on Finbar's shoulder, the Garda steadying himself. Finbar's body was pressed up against hers, closer than their bodies had ever been pressed before and continued thus while the Garda urinated against the wall. 'Good man,' he said then, was unsure where he had to go next, and let the downward incline of the lane decide for him.

She stole out again on the following night – she didn't have long, it was Christmas Eve – and they met under a tree inside the wall of the park. He gave her a fountain pen, a Parker. She knew that he must have stolen it, but she didn't care.

'Are you not afraid that I'll write you off?' she said, and she could see his head roll in amusement and embarrassment of this superstition about pens.

'Happy Christmas.'

He nodded, too shy of the words to return them.

She left first, swiftly, returning to the Square, head bowed to the light rain and to disguise herself. She slipped in through the porchway to the yard, got out of her coat and left it in a shed and, as casually as she could manage it, went in through the kitchen and up the back stairs. She would die for him.

Then, early in January, someone got Finbar a job as a messenger-boy in a butcher's shop, he lost interest in her, and her heart was broken for a time.

There was a new smell. Where was she? The fume of incense, was it? Grey light surrounded her. Where was she? The darting fish, the exploding and imploding ragged crows were gone to rest or dead, the ceiling had become flat, the fire, ashed, aged over. The mystery of her displaced self again in a colourless place, strange as in childhood when she used to lie motionless at night, waiting for Mom to come to bed, and wondering what on earth had she done wrong to be sent away. The small sounds from that other world, the kitchen, and sometimes a wail that seemed to come through the ages. Mom's innocent grief for herself. Sacred moments, feeling the darkness touch her open eyes, smelling it, tinged with the odour of ripe thatch as now with the grey dawn light that was filtering through the jaded curtain, suffused with the dissipating fume of the candle just gone out.

The sensation again of fainting, disappearing out of herself, even from her face, leaving her without feature or substance, to move out into the vast, colourless space. She rescued herself by pressing her hands, palms down on the bed, though, tonight, it was tempting to float willingly on. Because maybe she did not belong to anyone. Wasn't that a daunting thought? Maybe, like Mom, she didn't even like them.

'They're not nice.'

Yes, maybe, and a moment ago she felt a pride rising in her out of her refusal all those years ago when she was fourteen. Maybe she would defy them again. Was that the thought that was trying to reach her senses?

A clock was chiming in the distance. Six. It was two days since she had slept, her head was throbbing and the birds had started another day of bickering. She did not want to think any more, she

51

did not want to think at all and, good, that was the gate, there was the key scratching the lock. Come in, flesh, merciful sleep! And did she need something from her handbag or was she still ready? Let's see, heigh-ho, and touched herself again, put her fingers into the hole, the everything, the nothing, the reality! Naked came I out of my mother's womb and naked shall I return thither. Blessed be the name of the Lord.

VI

SEX

He barely glanced at her as he came into the room. His eyes washed the wall in an arc over the bed and he turned his back, unnecessarily, to shut the door. And, as if he had shrunk while he was out, the overcoat looked vastly too big for him.

'Mmmmm!' She stretched herself and inclined her head towards the wall to indicate that his undressing would be safe of observation.

'The dogs.'

'What?'

'They're out the back,' he said. 'Let me, let me let them out a minute.'

The misshapen coat left the room on weightless footsteps.

She heard the back door being unbolted and grating on the floor until it lodged itself. Now he was outside the window, coaxing two dogs, Cleo and Tina, out of a shed and taking them down the garden.

Chill, morning air drifted in from the back-kitchen. She had hoped that this one was not going to turn into a job but he had sobered up considerably. There was not much whiskey left in the bottle.

The rush of water hitting the sink yielded in squeaks to a trickle: he was back, putting down a drink for the dogs and having one for himself. One of the dogs, a greyhound, came in to stretch her back legs and yawn indifferently in Vera's direction before responding to the whispers growing more urgent to return. Cleo.

He was taking the dogs down the garden again.

These chores were understandable but, the dogs re-kennelled, the back door unlodged again and bolted, he was opening and closing cupboards out there, another drink of water, sniffling after the morning air and blowing his nose, a difficult cigarette to be lit: 'Op-pup-pop!'

Delaying tactics.

A flapping sound. Was he taking off his clothes out there? To and from the lavatory, 'Op-pup-pop!' The flapping sound again. If he had taken off his clothes, or some of them, was he putting them back on?

On average, Finbar got his hole about four or five times a year. Say, four. Two of these were opportunist's occasions: his turn with a right one, a ride in a doorway or in the back of a van – that kind of thing. And usually about twice with Florrie Delaney.

Florrie was a maid in the Sacré Coeur but she wanted to do better. You could see she wanted to get on in the world from the way she dressed. The severe colours, to be respectable. The almost black, gaberdine two-piece, the full of the collar of the white blouse outside, and the shiny black high-heels. There wasn't much more on her than on a bird. She reminded him a bit of his mother.

But Finbar would be standing on the Square with the lads and if he saw her going up the street to the church, about nine o'clock when it would just be getting dark, the head up, the popping walk, and coming down again, after the visit, on the other side of the street, just a little slower and the head not held so high, he knew she would be right for it.

When it happened the first time, it became more or less a twice-yearly habit. It had been going on now for about ten years, and no one knew.

Then, as she went down the High Street, he would have made some excuse to the lads about having some business to see to, he would go down the South Mall and slip into the Lane. Then there was Mullery's yard gate, rusty corrugated iron, the back of the butcher shop he worked in as a youngster. It was about eight feet high but he could scale it to unbolt it from the inside. Sometimes he cut his hands. A peek out then to look at her as she came up the Lane, and she would come in without a word and they'd have it off. Occasionally they nodded to each other in the street. He didn't give a fuck about her either.

He got his hole about a hundred times in his life but he had never been in bed with a woman, a real bed with four legs and bedclothes.

He came in in serious purpose from the back-kitchen, square-shouldered, spritely, still in his overcoat. He sat with his back twisted towards the bed and Vera and commenced to unlace a shoe, one hand.

'Mmmmm!'

His head came up, listening, his chin turned a sharp arc in her direction, 'Op-pup-pop!' on the cigarette: he wasn't falling for anyone's tricks. And, now that he had made that clear, he recommenced the business with the shoe.

Why had she come here? If there was a reason, her mind was incapable of remembering it. It was a mistake but there wasn't much she could do about it now.

She waited, ready with a grin. 'Did anyone fucking spot yeh?'

'What!' He whispered it at the shoe, incredulous. His head came up again. 'Oh now,' he said wisely: he wasn't falling for that one either.

And he had wet and combed his hair and arranged his quiff! He was frightened of her and she had noticed earlier that he could be touchy. 'What time is it?'

'What!' The 'what!' was silent. The unlacing of the shoe was suspended again. He was pointing an admonishing finger at the shoe and looking sidelong at it. 'The O'Tooles are nice people,' he said. 'Civil servants and supermarkets, running the Vincent de Paul and marrying gentry and the father born in a workhouse they tell me!'

She couldn't help it: she started laughing. Exhaustion was making her light-headed; his talking to the shoe was ridiculous.

'What!' Silent astonishment at the impertinent shoe. 'Op-pup-pop!'

'Whatever became of that plan of yours to become a musician?'

'Oh, I wouldn't mind that at all!'

'The saxophone, wasn't it?'

'I wouldn't mind that either! Marrying the gentry! But, of course, the gentry is broke. I mean, they must be, because Marcia O'Toole, that is, The Greek's missus, Mrs Henry Locke-Browne, is selling articles she's procuring from somewhere to my colleague in the antique business up the road there. A lady coming up here to the Punjab after dark! Like the wife of that Czechoslovakian president one time, taking to the back-streets of Prague, hocking gifts of state to Czechoslovakian dealers and cheap-jacks. But, at least, we know where the Czechoslovakian one was getting her pieces from: where is Mrs Henry Locke-Browne getting hers?'

'Heigh-ho!' She swung her legs out of bed. 'Let's have a drink.'

His eyes glanced off her bare thighs. 'I don't mind,' he said.

He cleared his throat and sat back in his chair, stiffly. The business with the shoes was suspended indefinitely.

She shared what remained in the bottle equally between them. He accepted the glass without looking at her. His eyes selected a spot on the wall and he fixed on it.

'Down the hatch!'

'I don't mind,' he said.

He took a sip and waited, confident of the outcome of the contest.

'You were telling me a few years ago that you were writing a book?'

'What?'

'A book about what goes on in the town.'

'Op-pup-pop!'

'And about the people in it.'

'Ooooh!' to his spot on the wall, a commentary on her cunning. 'Right children of Prague are the O'Tooles!' he said. 'A very important and upstanding family in this town, very holy, and they at one another's throats after the mother dying last year. What! To and from each other's houses, fighting like cats and dogs! To and from the hotel, stealing the furniture and objects d'art and blaming and sacking the staff for it all! The town is delighted. The wayward one, they're saying, Vera, inherited the lot over all their heads. Now, was she that wayward? So, in the initial stages of panic, it's understandable that they were out to get their share. But, methinks they've come to some arrangement of late because the tempest has died down among them. They'll get the wayward one yet, no half-measures.'

'Finbar – '

'And Tom O'Toole of Legion of Mary and weights and measures fame, short of going on the radio to broadcast it, has made it known to all and sundry that he'll be bidding for the place at the auction. And Mary Jane Mansfield, once his greatest foe, now his handmaiden, supporting him and his right to the place. A hotel, yes, but the family home as well and, with the clergy behind him and considering our history against the English, what man, or woman, will bid against an honest man endeavouring to get back the family homestead? He'll get the place for nothing.'

He winked shrewdly at his friend, the spot on the wall, and toasted it.

'Oh, they're out to rook the wayward one, screwing her, they are!'

Had she been alone and less tired she would have cried but, sitting here on the side of a frightened man's bed, what was the point in crying? All she wanted to do was inhale deeply, feel it fill her lungs and exhale slowly, but it seemed an impossible thing to achieve. Absently, she drew a blanket around her and draped the corners across her knees. Just because he did not know how to deal with the present situation did not give him the right to hurt her, to keep on wanting to hurt her. He was talking to the wall again; he had stopped only to take another sip. She did not want to think any more; she did not know if she could take any more; she had had enough for one day.

'I don't know yet, exactly, where the in-laws fit in, his majesty The Greek, Mr Henry Locke-Browne, barrister-at-law and friend of the working classes, but I'm working on it. Or the other fella with the straight white eyelashes, Mr Declan Mansfield . . .'

But what could she do? Even if the car were outside now, she didn't have the will to go anywhere. But one of these days, Vera, you'll have to stop being so stupid, you'll have to start pulling yourself together.

'Because it's my business to know the O'Tooles' business and everyone else's business in this town, and that's for sure, and their pedigrees, back to the Flood, the Deluge and beyond.'

She wasn't listening to him any more. He was a noise in her head, syllables merging with birdsong, so many small hammers torturing an anvil. She eased herself off the bed on to her knees and sat back on her heels, all the time looking at the dead fire, the mound of white ashes. Mom used to sometimes wear a shawl about her shoulders in the evenings and sit for an hour, maybe two, just looking into the fire. Mom used black turf; it reduced itself to red ashes. Mom's feet and ankles were often dusted red. Except in winter, she rarely wore shoes of any kind indoors.

She did not notice that the blanket had slipped from her shoulders and lay on the floor behind her, or that her lips were moving, forming silent sentences. Perhaps she was simply counting to herself. Or that he had stopped talking. She inclined her head towards him until the side of her face came to rest against his knee. She felt, again, that it would be such a relief to inhale, long and deeply.

'D'you want me to leave?'

Nothing for a moment. Then the side of him that she was leaning against moved fractionally in a paralysed tilt, his far shoulder rising and falling slowly in ambivalent reply.

'What?'

The shoulder rose slowly again but it did not fall.

'Will we go to bed?'

The shoulder came down, bringing with it a nod to Finbar's head.

She straightened up, finished the drink in an automatic way, one go, 'Excuse me a minute,' and went out.

After what she considered to be a suitable length of time she pulled the chain and returned. He was not, as she expected him to be, in bed, but he was sitting on the side of it in his underwear, his knees together. Without stopping, she climbed on to the bed from the foot end, removing her bra as she did so and her knickers as she wriggled under the blankets along by the wall. She would manoeuvre herself to the outside later. He was smoking another cigarette and was drawing on it in a futile way. She brushed the back of his arm with her fingertips, then down the string vest, plucking the mesh and touching his skin through the holes. There wasn't a pick on him.

'Oh well!' he said then in a kind of sigh, topped the cigarette, put the butt in his matchbox and placed it on the floor.

He backed himself on to the bed. She was ready with her arm

and when his shoulders came down on it she drew him on top of her. His breath caught in the moment of their bodies' coming together and in that moment, too, tired as she was, she wished that he were naked. Nakedness was part of it. After a moment he yielded to the softness, sinking down into her, his hands where they had fallen, on either side of her, his face in the pillow.

Let him lie there still until his breathing regularizes itself.

She stroked his neck, then down his back, each movement loosening the vest and easing it up about his shoulders. He was becoming aroused and she touched the side of his face with her lips, a silent 'shh' rather than a kiss, to leave it to her. Fingertips and the expanse of her hand in smooth caresses over his back, and downwards, her fingers easing their way under the band, influencing the underpants downwards. His hand came to assist her but she took it away and placed it on her breast, touching the side of his face again with her lips, 'shh', and again, in further promise that he would discover how peaceful it could be. But, though his head continued fixed, persevering in the pillow, the rest of him was becoming activity. His hand was frantic now, was clawing and tugging at the garment to be unfettered of it, his knees trying to scale her thigh, catching the flesh in scorching pains against the sheet, his knuckles knocking violently against hers, his nails catching her until, somehow, he was inside her. A few thrusts, a few spurts and it was over. His panting stopped almost at once, as if he was ashamed of it. And, after another moment, as if remembering it, he slid his body down hers and came out of her. His face had come to rest between her breasts, the bristles pricked into her. But it was over and let him lie there still for a little.

She doubted that he was disappointed. She doubted that he was anything because, only for the slight rise and fall of his chest against hers, he might not have been breathing. His eyes, she felt, were open, but looking at nothing, and it reminded her of the black children that you see in ads, looking out on a world they will never know.

She eased him off her to the inside of the bed and, in the same fluent movement, turned him on his side to face the wall. He was no trouble. Without having to look behind her, she reached back to the room and found the leg of the armchair. Then, when she had drawn the back of the chair up against the bed, she returned her body to his, her arm enfolding his shoulder, her breasts pressed against his back. Soon she would feel the delicate pull on her flesh, her skin adhering to his, as she inhaled, long and deep, the draughts of air that had been resisting her earlier. Long and deep, heigh oh-oh, bringing slow, smooth descent into sleep.

She hardly noticed that her breathing came in fits and starts, the shuddering aspirations of a child that has cried for too long. The chorus of birds was becoming distant. She was dancing in Atlanta.

VII

THE BROTHER-IN-LAW

Henry Locke-Browne came out of his house in Elm Park, walked the crescent of sycamores to the Newcastle Road and turned left to get to the country. Though he was an observant man, he did not notice the silver Merc parked nearby.

He took a ramble of a couple of hours' duration every seasonable day of the year, always in the evening and always in the same direction, westward of the town. His family had once owned everything on the eastern side. The switch to Catholicism in his grandfather's time did nothing to arrest the declining fortunes and by the time Henry was baptized into the one true church there was barely enough land to sustain a couple of horses; before he was out of his teens, that too was possessed. A German lived in the Big House now in a reclusive sort of way for part of the year. It was a matter of indifference to Henry, he told himself, who owned the land now or who lived in the house but, lest these daily constitutionals be interpreted by anyone as regret for what was, he followed the sun.

The solitary walks allowed his mind to range, past and future, and to witness the phenomenon of the present. 'Hell,' he thought, walking the new bungalow-culture of suburbia.

'O Sybarite!' was how he was greeted one evening on entering The Thatch: this because of his habit of rising late and his leisurely way of life. It was the season of the Circuit Court, The Thatch was convenient to the Court House and he knew that colleagues from Dublin would be assembled there. Later, in the same festivity, another mendicant barrister referred to him as 'The Greek' and it stuck. He was pleased with the nickname, though naturally he didn't show it, as well as counting himself fortunate that the correct etymological evolution from Sybarite had been misjudged. It would have been intolerable to have been called The Italian.

But it was only rarely that he sought the company of his academic peers or the town's professional class for that matter. Mannions was his local. Predominantly, he mixed with the common, male populace, standing about on the Square with them and translating their simple interests into language close to the epigrammatic. He attended last Mass most Sundays, always arriving late and casually dressed to show that he was there only to hear the sermon which he would interpret later for the chosen audience and comment on the standard of English used. On a few occasions he had, with success, defended one or another of the local down-and-outs in the District Court. The judge would have welcomed his presence on a regular basis: he relieved the tedium of the courtroom.

Only the tops of the tallest buildings were visible behind him now; in the distance, up ahead, the bridge and, beyond it, the stained twin towers of a factory. Perhaps he would return by way of these landmarks, circuitously, and he took the winding lane that led to what once was Woodlawn.

Mama was buried in Kenya. When he was fourteen she had gone there, ostensibly on an extended holiday and to visit Daisy but, in reality, in protest against what had become her husband's life style. It was Auntie Lou's quiet money that had provided for the young Greek and, on her death, she left him her house in Elm Park, two silent Afghan hounds and half of her money. The other half went to his sister Daisy, the nun. But the past, when he thought about it, had more to do with his father than with any other member of his family.

He walked through Woodlawn, through the stumps of trees left behind by the saw-mill people and continued on, skirting the brambles, the nettles and cow-parsley that flourished in the rubble of O'Beirne Hall. It never failed to amaze him that even as a ruin it had all but vanished. The stones were gone, even those of the outhouses, carried away by the small farmers for whatever purpose. Back to their place of origin, perhaps, to fill in the hole again. These were an active people with a passion for levelling things.

The path, beaten by his own feet, led towards the river and he held his breath for a moment, hopeful of the sound of flowing water. He had courted his wife here, Marcia, and, before that, her sister, Mary Jane. They had looked at their feet, at the moon and the stars and listened to the water, chasing itself around and over the stones. Mary Jane was some kind of nervous stick now, with a criminal's mind. But he had touched her breast one night and immediately she started to tremble. As if she had been waiting for his touch, every fibre of her being became alive in an instant. She stepped back, her eyes brimmed with tears, a maiden's blush, but her hands were open to him. So excited by the palpable sexual vigour of Mary Jane that, that night, he could only wonder at her. Later they laughed in celebration of the discovery. What happened to it? He followed the path to the river. She had sublimated it through greed.

His father had a taste for Bushmills whiskey and young women, women all-sorts. Behaviour that the locals would have found difficult to countenance in one of their own could be celebrated when relating to the gentry. A favourite story in the town was of the parish priest arriving at his father's door and demanding that the young woman, then living in the house, be despatched at once to wherever she came from and cease the bad example that was being set to the whole countryside. His father replied to the priest, 'When you get rid of your housekeeper I'll get rid of mine.'

It was important to The Greek to consider that his father was remembered with affection.

He stepped into the sudden murk, forgetting how sudden, too, it became cold in the shadow of the mound that rose above him. He climbed the side of the mound and found the light again and the heat of the evening sun as he emerged over the ridge. Another mound ran along the bank on the far side and down between was the dark river, now as regular as a canal and as silent. They had deepened it. The sides were sliced, the bottom dredged and he was standing on the excavated rocks and earth, the river's amputated bones and entrails, and the heart, too, perhaps. The fields had been made bigger. Before this digging was done it wasn't even fit for growing – rice, a round farmer explained one evening; drained and cleared of gorse and ditches it would produce more grass for everyone. There was no argument to be put against the economic advantage. Equity, like nature, does nothing in vain.

But it was mostly possible to avoid the human encounter. Seemingly everything growing wild had to be rooted out and they kept their heads down. The occasions of inadvertent proximity were marked simply by a farmer straightening up, looking and then gargling something in his throat and, in pretext of deference to the industry, The Greek would flutter a hand at half-mast from his hip and pass by. He was a moving part of the landscape. Still, he took precautions and from the height of the mound he sniffed at the air, testing it for impurities, and surveyed the area again to determine the continuing route. Why are the Chinese slant-eyed? Because when they come down in the morning they say, Oh, Jesus, not rice again.

He used to watch his father secretly. He sometimes caught his father in unguarded moments, standing in the yard maybe, in forgotten purpose, the wiry frame sagged over the bent knees, mouth slack, frozen bewilderment under the heavy, unmoving eyelids. Father was aware of him too of course and the tips of the fingers to the stubble, a message to the jaws to brace themselves, to thrust out the chin, and upwards to find the sun and grin lecherous teeth back at it. Two silent men — well, a man and a youth — sharing a few summers in the Big House, neither of them demonstrating their mutual respect and affection. A son did not take the lead in such a matter and for a father to have given open expression in word or gesture to his deep emotion would have shown a weakness to the enemy. Both of them knew that fortune and any idea of family were now utterly in decline and the question was how best, as principal players, in these the last stages to deal with it. The young Greek had not as yet discovered a strategy; the father, instead of bowing obeisance, waiting for the final blow — whatever that might be — went out to meet it, laughing defiantly, though the outcome was predestined. He had seen his father actually smash the stirrup-cup and drink from a bucket! His father had gone out as a jousting knight; tilted from his horse, he still got up to drink again and laugh further at destiny. O mio babbino caro!

The present returned, borne on a zephyr. Why doesn't slurry constitute a health hazard in the way that human excrement similarly disposed of will cause typhoid? Because it is mainly only grass perhaps. He had been planning to cross the river and return to the town by another route but on the slopes near the wooden bridge, silhouetted in front of the setting sun, a tractor was pulling a fat tank that was disgorging itself of a relentless black hail. He would have to return by the route he had come. Truly, the shit was hitting the Great Fan.

But when they seldom come, they wished for come, and nothing pleaseth but rare accidents. There were exciting moments, rare,

THE BROTHER-IN-LAW

when father invited son into his world, if only for a little, and the young Greek entered and felt privileged.

Father would put a bottle of whiskey on the table for them to share and music on the gramophone to the capacity of its volume. The gramophone to assault the silence about them; neither of them was musical. His father's grey intelligence contemplating the table, the stubble on his face like washed sand, the short coughs, the nervous cigarette held in the tips of his fingers. The young Greek was alertly appreciative and, in understanding of a father's concern for a son, would every now and again get up to wind the gramophone, to turn his back so that the father could take a second drink to his one.

Now the upthrust chin, father laughing with his breath, and the young Greek's delighted grin widening in response. The excitement of being together, they would fix on each other, eyes shining, grateful, fluid, but never forgetting that what they were sharing was defiance. That was important.

When there was a finger left in the bottle, two at the most – nothing in quantity to damage a sixteen-year-old son – father would get up. He would stand in the doorway, jigging a dance on the bent knees as if in comic urgency for the lavatory, arms weaving open circles about his head, eyes protectively reduced to slits, and go out. And the young Greek would wait to hear the Land-rover or the horse's hooves on the drive, his grin disappearing to nothing. His father, the aging Ulysses, was bound for Nighttown. Then he would get up and play once more whatever was on the turntable. 'Trees', 'Silent Worship', whatever. The songs in themselves meant nothing, of course; well, perhaps, only in that they belonged to Mama. But, o mio babbino caro, though loneliness is not without warmth, one of these days I fear that you too will not return.

The sun was going down and he was returning along the country lane to join the Newcastle Road. He was feeling very well. He had had a more than usually pleasant walk this evening and he had met no one. It was not that they were unfriendly, and their eyes were slow-moving, but in unprejudiced observation, he told himself, they were a shapeless people of indeterminate age; there was not a single handsome man or good-looking woman among them. Extraordinary.

The past merited being regarded as minor tragedy in that it had produced minor heroics. His father had entered a contest knowing that he would be beaten but, by offering defiance, carrying it through to the end, he would not be completely beaten. He had died in the Nighttown of the Punjab in a house owned by a Mrs Scarry. Apparently, there had been a move by some of the other occupants present on the night to remove the body and place it elsewhere but a daughter in the house prevailed successfully against the suggestion. (The Greek had come to know the young woman and had considered approaching her to express his gratitude, but had not done so, of course.)

The present was unspeakable. One salvaged what dignity one could from the present by refusing to participate in it. Indeed, contrary to an earlier opinion about his sister, he now considered that Daisy, as a woman, had chosen well in becoming a nun. The Greek was not going to be beaten, not completely, not at all because, consciously and deliberately, he was not playing. This was not passive resistance; this was sacrifice. He had decided to sit out his generation. It was the only course of action that he could see to ensure a decent future; the principle inherent in his sacrifice would influence the next generation. He had six children, the eldest of whom was a male child. The Greek was preparing the way; the family would be restored to name and influence through Norman.

'Hello! Hello! Henry!'

'Hell!' He was back in the suburbs. He was not, after all, going to be allowed to complete the course in the peace of his own company.

His wife was coming down the hill from her brother's house in erratic, short steps, both pushing and braking the pram. She had grown, largely, to respect his privacy and, apart from a hoarding instinct, like that of a child or a squirrel, and a tiresome inclination to dramatize the domestic incident, she was good-natured at bottom. But she should be at home at this hour, giving the children their supper and putting the youngest ones to bed. Why she should be out, leaving Norman to baby-sit his sisters, neglect his homework and his reading, was not acceptable.

Marcia was already shaking her head in her urgent approach, declaring that she had very good reason to be out.

He recognized the fresh alarm about her and turned his head in the other direction, his arm held out to the steep incline until the pram came to rest in the palm of his hand.

'Did you hear the news?'

'Tck!'

'No,' she said. 'Did you not hear?'

'What?' He spoke lightly, almost musically.

'Vera.'

'Yes?'

Her face slackened. 'Did you hear?'

'I didn't!' He turned his head to her, sharply.

'Lord!' And she was the one who was now looking into the dusk.

'Is she dead?' said The Greek.

Marcia's face began to slacken again: superstition of his last remark. The Greek shut his eyes.

'She's living with the tinkers!' And, to point it, she anchored her chin abruptly in her shoulder.

The Greek refused a reaction.

'In this town,' said Marcia, 'in-this-town, living with the tinkers! Henry! With that old thing, with that old sponger, that old lay-about, Reilly, Finbar Reilly!' She was near tears. 'Up in the New Estate.'

The Greek opened his eyes.

'Yes!' she said. 'Reilly, the medal man! That old trick-of-the-loop, that old – '

'In the Punjab?' said The Greek.

'In the Punjab, in the Punjab! Weren't the guards up there! Because of the car! Someone reported it – Didn't I see them myself walking round it and writing down the number!'

'What car?'

'The car, the car, the car, sure!'

'Hold, child,' said The Greek. 'What car?'

'The big silver one! Hasn't it been parked nearly outside our own front door for the past three days! No one knowing whose it was or how it came to be there, someone reported it to the guards and they traced it to Dublin. They found it was rented to Vera in Dublin – Hertz! Don't you know the way she is and, sure, it must have cost her the earth! How could the guards or anyone have known if she was alive or dead or kidnapped, Tom said. Then someone had seen Reilly skulking the back-streets near us, early the other morning, and the guards went up to him and there she was! Then the Super thought that Tom would like to know. Tom is in a desperate state. Then Tom drove up – ' Marcia was weeping. 'Tom drove up and d'you know what she did?'

He gave her a moment.

'She was in her underwear.'

'Yes?'

'Slammed the door in Tom's face!'

'Yes?'

Her face was swollen and wet with tears. 'Pardon?'

'Is that it?'

'No.'

'Yes?'

'I was going down for Norman.'

'Norman?'

'They want to see him.'

'What has Norman got to do with it?'

70

Marcia licked her upper lip for the answer. 'Vera has always given him money?'

The Greek shook his head.

'The Tin-Tin comics she sends that she reads herself?'

He shook his head.

'They've written a letter?'

The Greek nodded.

'It's urgent – it's very urgent – and they were saying that if Norman took it up to her she wouldn't slam the door in his face. They want to talk to her.'

The Greek shook his head: no Norman.

'Who are they?' he said, and when she did not appear to understand the question, he nodded at the hill. 'Who's up there with your brother?'

'Mary Jane.'

He shook his head again, this time absently. Norman was not allowed to become involved but his own attention continued on the hill: the situation was not without interest to himself. He came to a decision and, before starting the ascent, he gestured to Marcia to go home with her pram.

She set off obediently but when she felt that it was safe to do so, she stopped to look back at him, to admire him unashamedly. Yes, he was right to put his foot down over that starchy diet. Look at that figure, and he was forty-one; the straight back, the intelligence in that head; masterful; one hand elegantly in his trousers pocket, the other twiddling a daisy that he had plucked on his walk.

The tan leather patches that she had made with her own two hands and sewn on the elbows of his jacket at his request were now disappearing into the dusk and, as she stood there, she started to weep again with the pride that she felt in herself.

71

VIII

BELLEVUE HEIGHTS, CNOC MHUIRE

Caitriona, Tom's wife, answered the door. She was very pretty; petite. People used to stop to look at her as a girl, 'the doctor's daughter'. She was wearing a long, black, Arab wedding-dress with the square of bodice hand-done in coloured threads and beads. She appeared strangely young. She had lost herself again, temporarily. Her movement was beautiful, short steps that did not appear to touch the floor; perhaps she was wearing slippers or was in her bare feet. She stopped to look at the sitting-room door, to tell The Greek where he should go, and then went on, a silent mourner in innocent search of herself.

Mostly, she and The Greek got on well. As in-laws, an empathy, born out of their investment in the same family, existed between them. But it was obvious that she was heavily sedated at the moment. She suffered from her 'nerves' which, in turn, created a drink problem. The Greek knew that gin or vodka, it didn't matter which, were her tipples.

He knocked on the door and the conversation in the sitting-room stopped immediately. The floorboards shivered under the carpet: Tom's enthusiastic step. Even indoors, Tom overcame inertia by launching himself, head first, into motion. There was an innocence too about Tom.

Tom looked surprised to find The Greek in the hall but in the next moment he was sad. That was the way he was. The solidarity of a family in trouble moved him. He unclenched his fist and brought it up slowly for a handshake. The Greek was prepared for this: he bowed, and kept his hands behind his back.

'Come in, my friend,' said Tom, stepping back like a trained usher.

Mary Jane was sitting at a table in the bay of the window, smoking a cigarette. She too was surprised to see The Greek; they were expecting Norman.

'How are you, Henry!' she said brightly.

'I am very well, thank you, Mary Jane!' said The Greek. 'And you?'

'Very well!'

'Will y'have something?' said Tom.

'Ahm!' said The Greek, pressing his lips as in anticipation.

Normally, at this hour, he would be taking his first pint in Mannions. He drank three pints of an evening, sometimes a fourth if he chose to stay on after closing hours. Then, at home, he enjoyed a couple of whiskeys, Bushmills, Green Label, single malt. He binged twice a year, usually in Newcastle and sometimes to the point of hospitalization. Indeed, he had been feeling the symptoms of the next one coming on for the past week or so. But he had no intention of taking a drink in Tom's house. Tom was a scoundrel and The Greek was going to make him uneasy from the outset, that is, if he could penetrate the thorough-going hypocrisy. Hypocrisy is its own protection.

'What do you have there?' he said, elevating his chin to pitch a glance at the gilded trolley in the corner. Tom had no sideboard.

'Oh, there's!' said Tom, springing across the room and coming to what looked like a dangerous halt. 'Whatever y'like sure!'

'I beg your pardon?' said The Greek.

'A drop of sherry? It's dry enough, isn't it, Mary Jane?'

'Tiny gin,' said The Greek, drawing the corners of his jacket about him, preparatory to sitting down.

'A-a-a!' said Tom.

'I'm sorry?'

'I'm out of gin,' said Tom.

'A vodka will do nicely then.' And he prepared again to sit, to talk pleasantly to Mary Jane.

'A-a-a!'

The Greek frowned disbelief from the uncomfortable half-sitting position.

'A bottle of stout, a beer, a – '

'Bottle of stout,' said The Greek, dismissing the matter, and sat down. 'Well, Mary Jane,' he said, 'you *don't* look very well.'

She was a better match for him. To think that she once had a crush on this parasite. She smiled. 'Nice walk?'

'Beano!' said The Greek. 'And young Declan?'

'He's fine!'

'D'yeh want to pour this yourself?' said Tom.

'No,' said The Greek. 'Groceries selling well, Mary Jane?'

'Dandy!'

'Well, ye're a nice pair the three of ye,' said Tom, ''twas morning last night when ye came in. Now if this's to continue it'll have to stop 'cause if ye want to stay here ye'll have to go somewhere else!' showing that he, too, could be a good sport. 'The landlady, bejakers!'

Down below them the lights had come on. The window commanded the entire bowl of the town.

'Now, my friend,' said Tom, setting the glass of Guinness in front of The Greek, and he sat down. 'God bless!' He crooked an arm over the back of his chair so that his body should not slide under the table, and sighed. 'Yeh heard,' he said then.

Cattle, thought The Greek. 'I'm sorry?'

Tom shook his head at the table and his finger tickled the underside of a sealed brown envelope that lay before him. 'Well, if this's what the world is coming to,' he said, 'I don't know where it's going. If this's what we're bringing up our children for.' He sighed again. Then he looked wistfully at The Greek. 'Can anyone explain that to me, Henry?'

The Greek glanced his concern for Tom at Mary Jane and for an interpretation.

'Vera,' said Mary Jane.

'Vera,' said Tom to the table.

The Greek let them see that he was trying to understand them and he considered it, 'Vera,' silently.

'You met Marcia,' said Mary Jane with a trace of annoyance.

Yes, he had met her and, 'something about delivering a letter,' he said and other everyday matters, but he was baffled – he showed them the palms of his hands – as to what had produced the air of grief.

Tom was jacking himself up in the chair. 'Did Marcia not tell you where our sister is presently residing?' he said hoarsely.

The Greek nodded, yes, thought about it and nodded a second time that he was sure of it. 'But what is the problem?'

Tom was incredulous, his mouth growing and freezing a silent 'What?'

The Greek turned an attentive ear.

'Ut?' The 'what' became vocal. Tom could sound certain words, almost, without moving his lips.

'Henry – ' said Mary Jane.

'Ve-ra!' said Tom. His face was mobile again. 'Don't yeh know what she's doing to us sure? Ve-ra, Ve-ra!' A singsong. 'She's us in a flaming pickle, we're in a moral fix!'

The Greek continued rapt attention on him.

Tom's incredulity again, this time the mouth elongating to fix itself in the smile of a comic mask, grotesque.

'Cigarette?' said Mary Jane.

No, The Greek didn't want one but he invited her to share his fascination of her brother. He nodded to Tom.

''Era!'

'Vera?' said The Greek and when Tom nodded, yes, 'What age is she?' He reached for his glass but changed his mind at the last moment. 'She must be forty years of age,' he said and looked at both of them, eagerly, for confirmation of his estimate.

Mary Jane held up her hand to take charge of the discussion but, 'I don't know and I don't flaming care what age she is,' said Tom with passion, 'but she's old enough to know better than go disgracing herself and her family and her morals in this manner! And – lookit! – I'm as liberal as the next fella going but there's a flaming line. And – furthermore! – what's wrong is wrong. Is diabolical. It may be the seventies – even if it was the eighties, the twenty-first – or! – the twenty-fifth century for that matter – I would be astonished! And! – Henry! – I, for one, refuse, cannot, cannot, refuse to turn a blind eye. My conscience.'

'Don't follow,' said The Greek.

'She's thirty-seven,' said Mary Jane and, on the pretext of tossing her hair, she shook her head at Tom to warn him that The Greek was playing with them.

But Tom's only impetuosity was in homily and he was off again. 'Values! . . .'

There was a gleam in The Greek's eye that Mary Jane didn't like. He liked to play games but she felt that she was more than up to him. Just because he or his kind could not lord it over people any more, what else could they do but hang about the Square with 'the lads'? If he was any good would there now be a German living where he should be living? Declan would buy and sell him. His condescension and his big words. What else had he? A few social graces and a daisy in his hand! Don't forget I know him, she told herself. But they needed him, or, at least, they needed his son, Norman, so let him play his little games for a minute.

The letter had to be delivered to Vera. Tom could not go up to the New Estate a second time. Obviously, he had said something stupid that he had not mentioned, making Vera dig her heels in and had shut the door on himself. And Mary Jane was hardly the person to go up to that place. She'd die! To stand on some knacker's doorstep, smiling, talking to her eldest sister in her underwear! There was Declan, of course, Mary Jane's husband, but this one needed something more in style than whistling, telegram-boy delivery. No, this was a job for a child. Vera could be as thick as a mule but she was sentimental. The innocent appeal of a child's face, the touch of tiny hands in a transaction. It was a pity that Tom's children were away, temporarily being cared for by their granny; all three of them could have been dropped up there. Norman was the best idea.

'Excuse me!' said Mary Jane.

'Well, not if my life depended on it! And – Henry! – furthermore . . .'

Tom was playing it his way, the only way he could play it. His strength was in his ability to believe, utterly, every word he himself said, while another part of his head slowly worked out the real problem. And there were times when Mary Jane watched the process with an interest close to admiration but, presently, he was getting on her nerves and she wished that he would stop the, frankly, bullshit.

She extinguished her cigarette and lit another one. The plaster ashtray was shaped as a slipper and had a sleeping puppy flopped across it. There were seven cigarette butts in the slipper. She was definitely giving them up when she got The Wool Stores.

She had agreed to play ball with Tom. Tom, flanked by Mary Jane and Marcia, would attend the auction for the hotel: Tom would bid for it and secure it, unopposed, for a figure between thirty and forty per cent of its value; applying the same differential,

Mary Jane would then purchase The Wool Stores off Tom. (And Marcia had been promised the jewellery, trinkets, for her part.)

A conditional contract had been drawn up between them. On Mary Jane's recommendation, figures, ie, valuations and percentages of valuations of the two properties involved, were kept out of it. 'Just in case,' she said. Instead, the relative values of the properties were represented by a ratio. 13:1. She had also suggested that the two properties should not be called by their names but be expressed as x and y in the contract, though she knew that this was a nonsense, a legal impossibility. But she had her reasons.

Tom was incredibly cunning but he wasn't very bright. So was Tommy Martin, his solicitor. Tom would buy the hotel for himself at a fraction of its value, then he would get grants off the Tourist Board to do it up, and then he would sell it at its full, new value to the limited company she suspected he had formed with his solicitor, or he would just sell it.

This was already taxing his brain-power but, just in case, and to ensure that his mind did not dwell on the figure she would secure The Wool Stores for off him, she kept the matter complex by throwing in every bit of mathematics she could muster. She had worked it out that Tom would buy the hotel – at a fraction of its value – for between £55,800 and £74,400: therefore, working the differential, she would buy The Wool Stores off him for between £4,200 and £5,600, plus she would pay his stamp duty on what he paid for the hotel. Not bad. And she had it in black and white, binding, cast-iron. One had to protect oneself.

Well, wait until you see what he will do to Vera. On the sale of the hotel, Vera should receive a sum of between £55,800 and £74,400 from Tom, but don't make Mary Jane laugh. Though Tom did not know it yet – he really didn't – he would give Vera a thousand or fifteen hundred pounds, just to get her to sign the deeds – yes, promises, and tears, too, that when he did this, that and the other, she would get the rest of it – and that would be that.

But that was none of Mary Jane's business: when that time came, Tom and Vera could dance together naked on the Square, for all Mary Jane would care. Mary Jane, when that time came, would have given up smoking and be getting a decent night's sleep at last because she would be the owner of The Wool Stores. That is, all going well, she told herself, if you see what I mean.

But Vera had come back and to what extent this sudden and inexplicable return jeopardized the plans was hard to determine. They had to contact her and get her out of the New Estate, where people were up to every trick in the book, with all celerity. She had learned the word from The Greek.

'So! – Henry – ' Tom was saying.

Mary Jane pushed the ashtray from her, noisily, across at him. 'Excuse me!'

'Yeh see!' But he was about to rest his case. His knuckles rapped on the sealed brown envelope five times. 'We have to save her.'

Mary Jane was about to address The Greek when she realized that the door had opened and Caitriona had come in.

The movement of a sleepwalker. She drifted to a stop. She stood for a moment and smiled at them, a memory of the past. Then she went out again.

Tom looked up. 'She'll be all right,' he said.

Mary Jane smiled sympathetically at the closing door and, out of respect, decided to give it a moment before talking to The Greek.

The only sound now in Bellevue Heights, Cnoc Mhuire, was the rhythmic click of paper on plaster. Tom was looking down again, dealing thoughtful blows with the hard edge of the envelope to the head of the sleeping puppy that decorated the ashtray. The letter would be delivered by Norman, but that was only one move. What else should they be doing? What about a call to Father Billy?

'I just had an idea,' said Tom.

'Excuse me!' said Mary Jane, blinking in order to dilate and flare her eyes the more at him.

Well, bless my innocence, said Tom to himself, thinking he had got the message. Fair, flaming dues to Mary Jane. So that was why The Greek's attitude had been puzzling him! Here Tom was, discussing decadence all evening and, considering the history of the Locke-Brownes on that score – tally-women, sure, orgies, flying right, left and centre in the face of mother church! – he had been embarrassing Henry. He smiled privately from his resumed slouch at Henry, God love him. And he was thinking fondly of his other sister, too: for all her simplicity, she'd make a man out of Henry yet, God love her, Marcia. Leave it to Mary Jane.

'You can imagine our surprise, Henry, at hearing that our sister had returned,' she was saying, 'let alone hearing where she was living. Hearing it from the police? Marcia was particularly upset, I'm sure you noticed.'

The Greek, poised, nodded to her to continue.

'Well,' said Mary Jane, joining her hands to think for a moment. There was something about The Greek, out of the usual, that was hard to fix. 'Vera,' she said, 'doesn't mean to be irresponsible. Though she doesn't know it herself, she's headstrong, and she's easily led. She can be difficult to deal with. She has, though, always responded to children and she has always had a special affection for Norman, and I don't blame her.'

The Greek smiled.

'Hmm?'

'Oh no,' he said silently, only shaping the words.

'What?' said Tom.

'No Norman,' said The Greek.

Mary Jane gestured to Tom to forget it, her eyes on The Greek. Declan would do the job. What was The Greek smiling at? Some instinct made her uneasy.

'I understand,' she said. 'It's always difficult for in-laws in these little family affairs. Tom, Marcia and I, the immediate family, are of course the ones to deal with it. But it was very good of you to call.' She sighed, 'Well!' her contented resignation and gratitude, indicated that the interview was over and that he could be on his way.

The Greek sat back in his chair.

'Hmm?'

'Good health!' He picked up his glass, toasted them, and tasted the flat Guinness.

He was smiling at himself. What had attracted him to the O'Tooles was the idea of family. Mary Jane's enthusiasms about Daddy and Mammy and Tom and her sisters, domesticity filled with routine trivia, with rivalries and loyalties and innocent banter across the table, so hugely attractive to the young Greek that he considered the O'Toole family was warmth itself.

But Tom had said something and it was the moment that The Greek had been waiting for. 'But what are we to flaming do with this?' he had said, holding up the sealed brown envelope.

'I'll deliver it,' said The Greek, standing. The envelope was in his hand.

'But!' said Mary Jane.

'Not at all,' said The Greek.

She was on her feet and he was smiling down at her. Marcia was a good-natured woman and Norman and the girls were growing taller by the second. Mary Jane would have given him water-carriers.

'When?' said Tom.

'The very first thing when I rise tomorrow afternoon,' said The Greek. And since he already knew two of the sisters, why not Vera as well? After all, in behaviour she was the most aristocratic of them.

'But!' said Mary Jane again.

'For you!' said The Greek, presenting her with the daisy.

And left.

IX

THE MEDAL MAN

Vera was gone, bag and car keys, and there were two and a half thousand medals scattered everywhere about the room. He had no recollection of her saying goodbye, of how or when she left.

He had awoken twenty minutes ago, entirely naked, found the track of a welt on the crown of his head, dressed and had a look at himself in the mirror. There was a bottle, maybe two, smashed in the grate, objects that normally sat on the table were on the floor, and the medals everywhere. Something must have happened. They were even in the bed that he was sitting on and he removed one from under him, the Blessed Virgin. Idly, he flipped it in the air, then he forgot to catch it coming down.

He knew that the medals numbered two and a half thousand because he paid a hundred pounds for them, fourpence each, to the man in the pub in Cabra, in Dublin, a Sunday morning about a month ago, after a good night at the dogs. He did not have the strength to start picking them up. The silence in his head was like chilblains.

He knew that he had five hundred of her, five hundred mixed – All-Saints was written on the box – and fifteen hundred of the Pope. Some of the purple boxes were trampled on over near the door. There had been five boxes in all. Normally, a few pounds-worth of the Pope were enough for the season but he had dreamt that the Pope was going to be shot this year.

He could remember, from way back, losing money on his projects, on horses and dogs, for paying heed to a dream, a hunch, or for being superstitious, though it wasn't always the case, but he could not remember last night.

Drink has that effect on you, he told himself. Then you find something, a matchbox, you discover you are broke, a black eye in the mirror, and the story comes back to you and before it ends you might be glad of the black eye, gladder still that you are broke because it might teach you a lesson for a while. Or you might wake up to such a sense of loss that all you can think about is getting into a boat to cross the ocean to find the lovely woman, until you realize it was only a fucking dream you had and that, no matter how heavy your heart, you have to get on with your business. Isn't that the way of things?

This morning, though, in spite of the welt, the lost hours continued a black hole in his mind. For the moment he would have to wait on his memory, stay quiet, and hope that whatever happened was not punishable in a court of law. It was possible that he was still drunk.

The Pope had a thin-lipped smile and he was frowning mildly at his own infallibility. Finbar was about to pitch him, too, in the air when he thought, I'll go down on my knees and start picking them up, one by one. Maybe something will come of it.

He placed three of the cardboard boxes near him on the floor and he started the sorting. He sighed, remorsefully, over what he did not know. The All-Saints appeared to have hit the area around the fender because, for the first three, he got a St Anthony, a Child of Prague and Blessed Martin de Porres. Then, in a handful of five, he got two St Josephs, two St Anthonys and a Little Flower. He discarded the Little Flower and picked another one to see if he could make it a house. No improvement, another Little Flower.

He had always done a line in medals, he played with them in the cradle, he sold medals with his mother. 'They're clean,' she said, 'and you won't break your back carrying them anywhere and you can bless them yourself.' She was a cross little woman.

The quality of medals, though, had deteriorated since his mother's time. They were mean, paper-thin; the edges would cut you, they were only fucking tin. Maybe that was why, through a brilliant stroke of genius last year, while he was making two-headed coins, sweating them together with solder, that he hit on the idea of treating medals.

Wait'll you hear, he told himself.

The first thing you did was drill a bigger hole for the chain. That was an important first step. Then you put a dab of grease on the faces. From experimenting he found that a bit of dirt in the grease produced an even better end effect. Then you left them immersed in a tray of strong vinegar for half an hour. You took them out and washed them, being careful not to rub the faces. All but the faces were sparkling now and you dried them. Now another dab of grease on the faces was advisable and now came the tricky bit, threading them on to a piece of string with, say, quarter-inch spacers that you could make out of drinking-straws between each medal, and you always kept the dirty faces vis-à-vis. A tweezers was handy. You had your tin of liquid flux ready and, now, a quick dip of your line of medals into it. Your tray of molten solder was ready too and now you hauled your line through it, submerging the medals at first, then half-submerging them, floating them on their backs on the surface, bobbing them. It depended on yourself, how heavy you wanted them, where you wanted the weight, the shape you were after.

There once was an ugly duckling! Beautiful, lustrous, plump, substantial globules surrounding Our Lady of Fatima reborn Our Lady of Knock, embedded in the silver surround, and having been left uncleaned so that the solder would not stick, the face peering out had a lot more character.

He made thirty-five of them, to try them out among his other wares last year and, depending on how long the lustre held up and on the eyes of an individual customer, he decided that he would let them go at between three pounds fifty and a pound fifty each. And dependent on the moment, also, was what he would ask for a chain, if they wanted one. You could understand it if they didn't want a chain because these were lovely objects, for holding in your hand, for instance.

For his first sale he got four pounds off a girl for a pair of them and she was holding them up to her ears as she walked away, delighted. For his last one he got seven pounds off a nun from New Zealand. The thirty-five medals, for which he paid five pounds twenty-five, that is, fifteen new pence each, yielded one hundred and fifty-seven pounds fifty.

But here's where it gets interesting, how the medal-plan for this year came about. Wait'll you hear.

He thought he heard the gate. 'That must be someone,' he said, talking out loud to himself. The sound of his own voice brought him out of his reverie and he held his breath. Not the Guards again, he hoped. There was someone at the door, right enough, but the tapping did not have the authority of Guards in it and he crawled on hands and knees to the hall. He recognized the profile in the glass panel at once and the crew-cut.

'Not here,' said Finbar to the door, not meaning to have spoken at all and, in response to the next tap, 'Gone!' barking it, this time. I don't have to answer my door to anyone, he told himself, unless they come calling on genuine business. 'I'm not a maid!' he said.

'Pardon?'

Fucking pardon! People were cohabiting out of wedlock these

days all over the world and it was a well-known fact that these were not the Middle Ages, but he knew for certain that this whole business was going to end up with himself in handcuffs. The two fucking red-necks yesterday in their uniforms and squad car and, though he wasn't here himself at the time, Tom O'Toole after that. Then, in the evening, when the news had broken, there must have been a half a dozen aul' ones, in pairs, come up to see the house, the way aul' ones like to take a look at a place where a man has hanged himself. Now, and it was only gone half-eleven in the morning, Declan Mansfield of the straight white eyelashes was outside and he wasn't going away. Finbar could hear him whistling and poking the wares that were on display in the front garden with his toe. 'I'll have to go out to him,' said Finbar.

'That's a grand old bath, Mr Reilly.'

'Oh, I'm thinking of keeping that one for myself,' said Finbar.

'Isn't it a lovely morning, thank God!'

'Isn't it, isn't it, lovely! Thank God!'

'I'm sorry for bothering you at this hour,' said Declan.

'Not at all, not at all.' Fuck this. 'Vera O'Toole, is it, you're looking for, Mr Mansfield? She isn't here.'

Declan was a stocky butt of a fella and he looked athletically puzzled in his crew-cut and yellow v-neck pullover.

'Oh, she was here, all right,' said Finbar, 'but she's gone.'

'When?'

'This morning, early.'

'Where, Mr Reilly?'

I don't know nor do I care fucking-where Mr Reilly. 'Back, I suppose,' said Finbar. A fair and amiable guess.

'Back?'

'Where else?' He shrugged reasonably again. Then he raised his chin to look up the street, mild interest to see if anything was happening, leaving his face unattended for Declan's inspection.

'And that's a grand old table over there,' said Declan.

'That, would you believe,' said Finbar, 'came out of a castle in Scotland.'

'Oak, is it?'

'No, the rain has got at it. Mahogany.'

'See you around, Mr Reilly, keep the faith!'

'God bless!' Go and fuck yourself.

Before closing the door and going back to the medals, he took four of the bentwood chairs in the hall out of his fucking way and skyed them into the garden. Yes, let the fucking tinkers steal them on him! Only one of the dogs out the back was his, Tina. Cleo belonged to John-John McNulty, and he hadn't let either of them out yet for a piss. He was up for an hour and he hadn't even made as much as a cup of tea for himself to put something in his stomach. Fucking whiskey! An ulcer was only waiting its chance around every corner and worry was the worst fucking thing in the world to encourage it. John-John would take the two fucking legs from under you, very lively, if he thought you were trying to do him in any way.

Fuck the medals! He'd pick them up, if he wanted to, when he was good and ready. And he didn't want to remember last night, he wasn't interested, he didn't want to know or hear a single fucking thing about it from his head. He was being very unfair to innocent animals. He would take them out, past John-John's, for a good long walk. Whoever said it, if you stick to the pint you won't go wrong, was right.

He put the dogs on the leashes and went off with them. A breath of fresh air never did anything on anyone.

That O'Toole family was touched, the whole lot of them. And he was sure Vera was on something more than whiskey. There was an uncle – what was his name? – from out Glenora way, your man with the eye, the grandmother's side – Lally. He drowned himself in the barrel of water at the gable-end of the house. Lally wasn't his real name. His father was Darcy, a fiddler who went out to California.

Not that Finbar was unsympathetic, fair is fair. As a small child Finbar was down the town one day with his mother and a big man with a red nose and a handlebars moustache was coming out of Mick the barber's. 'How's young Finbar Wyvern then,' he said, 'eh?', gave Finbar a tanner and winked in a kindly way at Finbar's mother. Finbar went into it sufficiently later on to form the opinion that Finbar Wyvern had a truer ring to it than Finbar Reilly. So, as a rule, he avoided the subject of paternity as far as possible, even with himself.

And then there was Vera's mother. For all her twin-sets in angora wool and the spectacles on the fancy string, hopping on her chest, there was a fierce fucking peasant there entirely, underneath. Attila the Hun. And the size of her! But, no more than two of her daughters. Well, she started out as a skivvy in the Navarone Guest House, left it or was fired, took up the same position in the Imperial Hotel where Blessed Martin Joe O'Toole, conceived without sin, a born-in-the-workhouse crusader, teetotaller, non-smoker, non-consumptive, free of the palsy and all other indecencies, save one, his interest in the spiritual welfare of the maids, had her up the pole in no time at all. Let not thy right hand know what thy left hand is doing! And then there was the. Wait a minute, hang on. This was beginning to have the hollow ring of recent déjà vu.

He hadn't, had he, cast these charges at Vera last night by any chance? No. What? No. Well, he truly and sincerely hoped he hadn't because he was and he wasn't relieved that she was gone. He was feeling a small sense of loss. There was something nice about Vera. He hadn't had to put his hand in his pocket once and, even though it would have been no use had he had to, because he was broke, still. She had paid for all the drink, for everything, and, in cash, he was up eighty quid on her on the three days. For a woman who had travelled and who had, by all accounts, turned her share of tricks, which he was not going to go into, there was definitely something nice there, there was no other word for it, there was definitely something childlike. It wasn't right to have done her on the money. Those little starts that she gave in her sleep produced surprisingly tender emotions in him. He felt pity and fear for the two of them and warm at the same time. Indeed, there was one moment when he felt sad for the whole human race. Away back, something must have happened to the whole human race.

'Cleo – Tina!'

He wanted to interrupt this train of thought and he spoke harshly and yanked on the leashes. They were meeting the country air and it was making the dogs restive.

Well, something happened to fucking Finbar, he told himself, so, less of the nice stuff, allow fucking Finbar to stay with his stocktaking mind. I mean to say, is there leader in this town, fucking churchman or statesman, who wouldn't, given the chance of Vera, have done her worse? So, yeh see, that's the ethics of the piece.

But he knew that his mind was ahead of him, the fresh air had been working on it too. The reconstruction of events leading up to and into the lost hours had begun. With fascinated melancholy he stood back to watch his mind solve the mystery of the scattered medals.

'Cleo, Tina?' He spoke softly and drew gently on the leashes to bring the dogs close, one on either side of him.

Yesterday evening, yes, at home, right, it was about half-past eight, exactly, because dusk had started, they hadn't lit a candle yet and, what with all the riding and the drinking over the three days, wondering to see were the Guards coming back or Tom O'Toole with a posse on BMWs, and knowing that the neighbours in their curlers out cleaning the windows had a field day, two more aul' ones, linking one another for safety, had just passed by on the far side of the street, and you could see that they were going to turn to come back for another gawk at the place, the mesh of Finbar's nervous system was so tangled and electrified that he nearly took up the brush to go out and hunt the aul' ones. The trouble Vera had brought down on him! He would have to have a think about it all.

'I need to go out to get a few things,' he said to Vera. 'D'you feel like a fry? And I'll bring back a few bottles.'

She gave him more money, though, seriously, he hadn't mentioned money. She wasn't concentrating on what she was doing. He had a feeling all along there was something in her head that she was telling no one about, or she was trying and failing to work something out, and that she feared losing him.

Then he slipped out the back way, got over the fence, went down to the railway cutting and crossed it. He knew where he was going. There was a heavy dew coming down with the dusk and he felt it getting in through the cracks in his shoes as he crossed the Nuns' Field. If he was not mistaken, there was rain on its way. He was making for Church, Lar Begley's.

Lar's was a strictly no-credit-given pub. It was a strictly no-conversation pub also. There might be a whisper now and again but it was a rarity, an accident, and no one passed a remark on it. If a conversation was going on in your head, that was your own business. Likewise, if you wanted to let your mind coast, or have a break from yourself and not think at all, you could do so while still remaining, more or less, a part of the human race and, because of that, because you weren't in a vacuum like you might be, sitting on your own at home, it was the one place in the world where a man with a problem could think straight.

There were only six or seven people in the town who went in there and it was doubtful that they had ever attended all together on the one occasion. Some of the six or seven were known to hate each other in the outside world but they were safe under Lar's roof. In any case, people rarely smiled in Lar's because smiling, if you think about it, is idiotic. If another customer was present when you entered, even if he was your best friend, you just nodded and you left the man alone. Finbar hoped that the amateurs never got hold of it and came in to desecrate it with their innocence and ignorance. He hadn't told a soul that he called it Church. He went there about once a fortnight. He'd be lost without it. All you needed was money. The rest was simplicity.

Lar was deaf and, though it was known for certain that he was able to talk, he would not speak a word to anyone. For reasons known only to himself, he wouldn't have a hearing-aid. Maybe he was stone deaf and it would be no use to him or maybe he felt, in keeping with the vow of silence, that as he spoke none, he didn't want to hear any more shite-talk. No one knew what, if anything, was going on in his head.

The idea of Lar made Finbar remember that he used to think God was a submarine, coursing slowly forever the silent deep forty fathoms down and that, every now and again, when the eyes blinked it meant that a ping had gone off inside in response to one of Finbar's prayers.

'He's better than the word,' said old Stephen of Lar one night, taking the pipe out of his mouth, musing to himself.

But theorizing on the nature of Lar had ended years ago. It was enough for the seven who got drink there to believe Lar to be intelligent. Maybe they even loved him because, as Finbar read it, deep down there was a fear that somehow, some night, carelessly, someone of them would offend him and be punished. Which was a strange apprehension, because Lar neither liked nor disliked any of his customers and he couldn't be said to be happy or sad. He was out on his own.

The light, a single pendant, was on in Lar's and Finbar went in. There was no one at all in the place. Lar, as usual, was pointed in the direction of the street, leaning his left hip against the counter, the knuckles of his left hand pressing down on it, giving the upper part of his body all the support it needed. Below, in the gap cut in the counter, his right shoe was folded around his left ankle. Because he was very big he had to hang his head into his shoulder and this made the eyes screw upwards, giving him an unintentionally baleful look. That was the way he stood unless he was serving a customer. But if you ever saw him pointed in the other direction, that is, standing on the two feet and without any support from the counter, looking in the direction of the screen of coloured beads that his mother put up across the opening to the living-quarters one time, you knew that he was thinking of bedding down for the night and you had ten minutes. A child would understand it.

Finbar put himself in Lar's line of vision, showed his money and waited for the blink before putting it on the counter. If he didn't blink, you left. There was nothing to appeal to. He wouldn't ever serve a woman or any member of the Donnellan family, who were only blackguards anyhow, who came in now and again to see if they could win in some kind of silent contest against Lar. He always blinked for Finbar but Finbar believed that you should not take it for granted that he would.

Lar blinked and came to. Finbar put down his money, made the seven-inch gap sign between hands held horizontally for a pint of Guinness, pointed at the bottle of Paddy, followed by the three-eighths of an inch gap between thumb and forefinger, for a small one as well, so that he'd have something to be doing while the pint was settling. Lar wasn't very clean but alcohol was a disinfectant.

So, was he happy enough with what he had realized on Vera to date, should he explore the matter further, to its full potential, was his heart up to it or, left to his own resources, what were his prospects? He had gone the other side of the pot-belly stove and taken his usual seat in the alcove of a blocked-up doorway. Lar was pointed at the street again, his knuckles and hip using the counter. The pot-belly stove wasn't going that long but the puffs of smoke that it was making through the joints were diminishing as it heated up. Finbar nodded at the stove his awareness of how conducive the atmosphere was becoming for clear thinking.

Pre-Monday night, his life was the same as that of most other men going, with financial ups eventually being balanced by downs. His sexual arrangement with Florrie Delaney, he admitted, was primitive but you had to remember that he was a very simple man.

Faint heart never won a fair lady, and so say all of us, but what if you lost your senses in the winning and had to be carted away?

Since Monday night, when Vera O'Toole arrived, a complex of emotions had him questioning his very identity. The extremes of mood-swings he had experienced were only short of being incredible and wasn't the prospect of their continuing too much to endure? He had nothing but praise for the drink and the sex while they were happening, and the bit of money, but the hangover from all three filled him with dread and remorse and anxiety, impossible to understand, not to speak of his terror of the authorities taking sudden revenge. To rival it, a man would have to return to his time with the Christian Brothers in Letterfrack, where there was a graveyard with one hundred children, but Finbar was not prepared to go back to that. So, would he give Vera the gate, was that what he was saying? That was exactly what he was saying.

All at once it was as if a weight had been lifted from him. The brown-ochre paintwork seemed to glow and he noticed that the flagstones had been swept.

The door rattled and he craned his head to see past the stove-pipe who was in it. Dixie Shaughnessy was coming in and, without thinking, Finbar winked, how yeh, at him. Dixie looked through him. Finbar watched the ritual of the money between Dixie and Lar and Dixie giving a light downwards rub to an imaginary four-inch pole in front of him for his usual. Then, when he saw Dixie go to his corner with his pint of ale, Finbar went up for another round before Lar settled back again. You wouldn't ever want to over-work Lar and you avoided putting him through unnecessary coming-to motions. He felt safe for the first time in three days and, to celebrate, he had a double Paddy with his pint.

It was true that if you forget for a minute the money he was making on Vera O'Toole, he was broke. It was true that the year so far could not be called spectacular but, wait a minute, that was not to say he was reconsidering the decision about Vera of a minute ago. The year so far had not been without a few successes. The bentwood chairs. He had pointed John-John McNulty in the direction of a pair of mirrors he'd got wind of, in a place no one would ever think of, and for the tip-off he got a hundred and seventy bentwood chairs. He had spotted a man at the back of the dog-track an hour before the race, feeding a Mars bar to Stella Maris, the favourite, and he had put his shirt on Hearts Are Trumps, the second favourite, number 4, and won. He backed number 4 in the next four races and it came up twice, leaving him two hundred and forty-four pounds to the good on the night. He invested a hundred of it the following morning in a pub in Cabra in medals.

The scam with the ham rolls had only done middling but that was because he didn't have the readies at the time to finance the size of batch that would make it worth your while. If he let the cast-iron urn, which, he believed, was an original, go to your man who was pretending to be interested in the fireplace, he would have a right rake of rolls for the big match, Saturday week. He had his copy of the Almanac to consult for the dates of race-meetings, holidays, holy days, fairs, fleadhs, football matches. There were any number of scams he could think of and work out, not even including his furniture. Hats, T-shirts, Lucky Dip, scarves, rosettes, official programmes for any event, his camera for the seaside, lino for the buffers out the country, broom-handles for the pilgrims at Croagh Patrick, bodhrans, shillelaghs, for the Yanks, from Taiwan, not even including his ham rolls and his medals.

And if he hadn't done anything about getting them to reconnect him to the electricity, it was because they were saying that a sudden General Election had to happen and if that was the case there would be amnesties flying for everyone for anything from Mephisto O'Flynn. Something always came up! O Mephisto O'Flynn, you've a wonderful way with you!

Inside, he was singing to his prospects. And he was realizing now that the three-day adventure had the beneficial effect of shaking him up, making him eager to return to the familiar problems, to solve them and make money out of them, and it was good to have the feet back on old terra-firma.

The door rattled. That was Dixie gone out. Thursday night, he'd only have been having the one, all right.

Finbar realized that what he was drinking now and what he had drunk last night and the few he had today to settle him, after the Guards called, had started the ferment, making him prematurely drunk, so, in case he might forget them later, he would call a bottle of Paddy and a six-pack to take home when he called the next round in a minute.

He checked on Lar. Lar was chewing something. Sometimes, all right, you saw him put a handful of something into his mouth. Meal, Finbar reckoned, and that he had a bag of it beside the bed inside. He kept a few things by him on a shelf under the counter that his right hand could reach without disturbing the rest of his body. He kept three or four mugs there, all of them brown on the inside. But one of them had a picture of a robin on it and if he ever put it on the counter, whether he was using it to drink from or not, you didn't go near him until he put it out of sight again. You could approach him, however, when he was chewing and Finbar got another round and his take-aways. A twelve-inch vertical thread for the bottle of Paddy, the open jaws of a pincers pointing downwards for the six-pack.

He thought of his earlier beleaguered state of mind and his present happiness intensified. He signed for another round. What harm, hadn't he the place to himself! His mood was self-congratulatory now, in conversation with himself.

D'you know what I'm going to tell you? Wait'll you hear this.

Finbar was looking for a hammer under the sink and he found a medal. It could have been there since his mother's time. He didn't bother to look at the image, he just assumed it was the Blessed Virgin. He hadn't planned to do an experiment that day so maybe he didn't follow last year's procedures to a 't', which was what he wanted to do. But he'd found the medal, anyway, and it was the only one in the house as far as he knew, and he thought he'd see. Wait'll you hear. He drilled a bigger hole for the chain, he gave it just a lick of emery on the face, a good rubbing to the back and all round and over the rim. He hadn't used the emery last year, he let strong vinegar do the job, but he was out of vinegar.

Dominus vobiscum! He dipped the medal in flux, to promote the fusion, yeh see. Where's me grease gone, he says. Dab of grease from the sprocket-wheel of the bike on to the face of the medal. Et cum spiritu tuo! Now, lo, he baptizes the medal in molten solder, dips it, one, two, three times! I will go unto the altar of God, to God who brings joy to my youth! See him, how he floats the medal on the silver waters of Babylon! He's after a shape, something like a tear, a sort of globule.

Here's where it gets interesting.

Kyrie, Kyrie, he's twisting the string, he's watching the transformation, Kyrie! He's thinking, there once was an ugly duckling, when, hello, what's this? There was something going wrong. Lo, the solder was not falling from the greased and only partly-cleaned face, like it was meant to do, like last year. Christie-Christie-Christie! The shape of a globule, yes, but where was the Virgin Mary's face peering out at you, as from a silver cave. The medal was disappearing into the stone, becoming engulfed, it was gone. He hardly knew which was the face side now, it was like a small fruit, and he took it out. Ora pro nobis, he poked the string out of it and, as last year, there was a beautiful dimple, convexing smoothly to an orifice for a chain, unlike the mean, burred hole of the original but, so what, what use to anyone was a little silver pear? Dies irae!

But wait'll you hear.

He was about to see if there was another one, by any chance, under the sink when it started to happen. What's this, he says? Lo, two small black dots appearing in the stone, appearing to come from the centre to the surface of the stone! They are growing inside the stone, darkly, and coming to the surface. It was like an x-ray that you'd started to hold up slowly to a light.

Lo, what can these be, he whispers? Impurities? Or can it be a skull? The banshee is out tonight, go down on your knees and say your prayers! The line of a mouth had formed, the dots had become sockets, light and shade were creating strong brows over the sockets, eyelids, a chin, the high points of cheek-bones and deep creases curving down the cheeks from a strong nose.

Wait on, he whispers, oh, not without fear of what he was witnessing because this was not the track of the Virgin's face and, as true as Christ in the shroud of Turin, it was the Pope who was in it! What did you do? What did I do? What could I do but laugh and say, can this be another sign, because, that very instant, I remembered I'd seen the same man shot the night before in a dream.

But, listen, it isn't right to be smiling in here and maybe it's nearly time to gather up and go. You may think I'm drunk and I'll answer you back, I am. You may say dreams have let you down before and I'll say, so has everything else. You may tell me that signs are only wishful thinking but I'll tell you, the only thing likely to shake the Medal Man's conviction of ten thousand pounds out of medals alone, this year, will be a bigger and a contrary sign to the ones he's getting.

'Oh, Jesus,' said the sober Finbar to himself. At this stage he was in the football field where there was no barbed wire to hurt the dogs and he had let them off the leashes. He suspended the recollections of the previous night for a brief commentary. The recollections had given him a drawn, intelligent look.

'What kind of shite-talk at all do I go on with to myself in drink? What's all this shite about the Pope? The man can die peacefully in his bed for all I care.'

How did a hundred pounds-worth of medals get scattered all over the room was all he wanted to know. And he had simply told Vera that her time with him was up and requested her to leave, yes, given her the gate, that was all, wasn't it? His last remark was dishonest because he now remembered the moment of hitting Vera and he wanted to deny it.

He whistled up the dogs and he was grateful that they responded at once because he needed them. He crouched down on his hunkers to gather Cleo and Tina to him and bury the face that had become handsome in remorse in them. They licked his ears and his hands and the top of his head and their love moved him. 'I'm sorry, I'm sorry,' he said to them. He was back in Lar's, picking up the six-pack and the bottle of Paddy.

The hair was standing on the drunken Finbar's neck. Even before he looked and saw the way Lar was, he had sensed the change of atmosphere in the place. Not if it was a stone that was doing it could he have been more astonished, not if you had locked him up in an empty church at night and tied him to a pillar and a forest of statues were moving towards him with bleeding outstretched hands could he have been more frightened and awe-stricken. Now he understood why the tinkers never came near the place.

Lar was standing inside the counter, head hung, facing the screen of coloured beads, crying.

Finbar felt himself go pale, his eyes widening. 'Oh God!' he said.

And though he could feel an intense heat and he could hear singeing and he could smell burning hair, his feet were stuck to the floor.

'I'm sorry, Lar, I'm sorry,' he said and, again, the voice did not sound like his own.

Lar continued there, dumbly, head hung, facing the screen, with one big tear after another running down the side of his face. How long since he had reversed the stance to indicate that he was for bedding-down would never be known, but even if Finbar had exceeded the permitted ten minutes drinking-up time by as little as five, he knew that Lar's was finished for him now, forever. Then he realized that in the horror of the first moments of the experience he had backed away and the intense heat behind him was his coat, burning against the stove.

He only stopped to get sick and then he didn't stop again until he was halfway through the Nuns' Field. That he had forgotten the fry was the least of his worries and as for the thick rain that was coming down, fuck that too. He was a man, weak with fright, despised and rejected, and he went under a tree to sit on a stone and to open the bottle of Paddy.

He thought of his mother, God rest her soul, how she would pity his misery. Her bespectacled face swam up before him but she was gone again in a blink. Other white discs, like moths, the faces of people in the town, criss-crossed one another before flying up into the branches. Those were the people who considered him to be an enemy of their order. Stay, he said to their faces, to tell them that he was a threat to no one but himself, that the reason why he said fuck them was because he was frightened of every single one of them, that if only people knew it, he had a heart of purest gold.

It was a strange place for a man to be sitting, all right. He wondered were there pigeons up in the tree. He thought of a nice piece of cold chicken, he thought of Florrie Delaney, John-John, he tried to conjure a picture of what his father's hands were like, he thought of prison, his life, one of his own ham rolls. The confident dreams of an hour ago might as well not have happened. He had nothing, he was an outcast. At least the birds, if they were up there, had one another.

There would be no General Election.

It was truth time and his prospects were that he hadn't any prospects. I mean, if you take the ham rolls, the labour involved in ham rolls, I mean I'm talking hundreds of the fuckers, cutting them and cutting your fucking hands, messing and smathering with the makings, devising ways of stopping the fuckers going stale on you, soaking them in water, giving them their second baking to make them look fresh, sometimes having as many as three old cookers from the garden going in the kitchen at the same time, burning your fucking knuckles, blowing fucking fuses, paying a dreamer of a young fella to assist you, watching out for the authorities and inspectors, putting yourself under an obligation to John-John for the lend of his van. What? Fuck them!

And John-John did him on the mirrors. Them mirrors were worth at least a grand apiece. Bentwood chairs were worth sweet fuck-all, they weren't even fit for kindling. And he had reefed his leg putting his foot through one of them. If only he had bought the mirrors for himself. But, even if he had the money, he wouldn't have the courage. John-John would get away with fucking murder. Finbar wouldn't be so lucky.

And maybe this year they'll let no one but themselves within a mile of Knock, no closer maybe than Castlebar to Croagh Patrick. It was getting worse every year. The clergy wanted it all for themselves, then sending home the money to make more priests and nuns out of the young brothers and sisters. It suited them to pretend that St Joseph, a carpenter, wasn't Christ's father at all. They didn't give a fuck about the working man. The medals? He had as many pencils, razor-blades, grosses of all kinds of gewgaws upstairs that no one wanted, and upstairs, too, was where the medals were destined. He was finished. Unless he could think of some other use for them.

Those were his real prospects and the only subject worth thinking about was not life but reincarnation. He felt the tears well up. It was not his first time to think about reincarnation. If he had any say in the matter he was going to ask to be let back as a dog. There was nothing more beautiful in the world than to watch a greyhound. It was only a fucking toy that they were after but the single-minded way that they pursued it was beautiful, was pure, was heroic. It was the only thing that brought tears to his eyes.

It was dry under the chestnut tree, the branches came down in a canopy almost to touch the ground. But he had got a soaking out there and he was worried that he was not shivering. He wasn't the slightest bit cold but, more than likely, the feeling was false, a superficial heat brought on by alcohol.

What, at all, he began to wonder, was warmth? And he began to think of Vera O'Toole's breasts, falling on either side of her in the bed. She was massive. He never saw anything like it. How does a man describe breasts? And her hips, you could build a house on top of them. Then it came to him in a flash what he was going to do. He had it. He rose slowly, unconsciously, without apparent effort. He wanted to rush off but he checked himself and screwed the cap slowly back on the bottle. Are you sure you're not drunk? I'm positive.

Lo, see how fearlessly he goes!

The rain still came down as thickly as before but he laughed at it. It ran down his neck and he could hear it squelching in his shoes. For a man who fancies himself as being as wide as double-gates you can be very slow sometimes in seeing the obvious, he chided himself. The stumbling momentum had him almost running. He couldn't see himself as proprietor of the Imperial Hotel, standing in the doorway, looking out over the Square. The brother, the Mary Jane one or The Greek's wife would be taking it over, but there would have to be some kind of deal, the usual, and Vera wouldn't come out of the carve-up empty-handed.

Lo, see him, the bridegroom, hastening homewards through the night, over hill and dale, to his bride-to-be!

He slipped going down to the railway cutting but nothing was lost and he got up and crossed the tracks. He fell again going up the other bank and the six-pack came apart. He found the bottles, armed his pockets and his belt with them and he hurried on. He would sky the bentwood chairs out of the house when he got home, out of the hall and off the stairs. Let the tinkers have them! Now he was playing for real stakes. There was a double-bed up there, they might not sleep in it tonight because it wasn't aired but they might as well be making a start.

How would he go about putting it to her? That was the question.

He wasn't as shy of her now as on the first night but he suspected that he still wasn't up to her when it came to sex, what with all the y'know-stuff they got up to in New York. She seemed bored, once or twice, on the job. Still, he wasn't having anything kinky. He didn't have a ring but, wait on, he had it! He would bring her gifts of gold, frankincense and myrrh. And there was no bother on her, mind you, taking her clothes off.

He would lay his gifts at her feet. They would have a few drinks first. Her eyelids would be heavy and her dressing-gown hanging open. And he would lay the five casks at her feet.

Take off your robe, daughter, lie down on the bed and I shall make you whole again, I shall wash you in hyssop!

She lies naked on the altar now, her eyes are closed. She does not breathe.

He opens the casks and draws forth handfuls of the gold, frankincense and myrrh and he commences to cover her naked body. Kyrie, Kyrie! Slowly, he covers her with the silver discs of gold, frankincense and myrrh, head to toe, one disc at a time, yea, layer upon layer! Verily, yea, I say unto you, not even Solomon was dressed like this!

He leaves the mouth uncovered, yea, only the lips are revealed and, lo, now as a prince, a priest, a lover, he bends o'er her silver body to touch the lips in a kiss that will awaken her, shh! And, see, he breathes upon the mermaid to give her human form, shh!

First to move are the medals about her eyes. Lifted by her eyelids, they slide from her face. The maid was not dead but sleeping! Now she sees him, his frowning brow.

Rise, daughter of Jerusalem, thy faith hath made thee whole!

See her as the morning rising, shedding her mantle of silver scales, see what radiance surrounds her, choirs of angels and saints fall back from her and scatter, dazzled by her brilliance!

Her arms reach towards him, they strain to their creator.

Still, lo, he frowns. O ye of little morals, he groans, O ye of little faith, he moans, of many, many works and pomps, he screams!

Now she understands him and, naked as the morn risen, she bows her head in modesty and submission and puts her feet together.

Allelujah!

He waits to anoint her with his prize-piece. And now he fastens the silver globule about her neck. It hangs between her big breasts and he touches it with his lips, shh, as he stoops to kneel to kiss her feet. See how he kneels, his head bowed down, see his hands come up in homage, in adoration, to insert his fingertips into her sides. He presses gently down the blessed hips. She kneels beside him, vis-à-vis.

Daughter, many wicked men, it is said, have stripped you and defiled your nakedness but by this holy sacrament I have made you clean again and, from now on, you, my virgin, will be mine.

'Ah no.'

He was returning with the dogs. His step was spritely, he was square-shouldered and he was whistling, energetically, the same phrase of music, over and over. He would stop the whistling but, when he did, a frown tightened like a steel hoop around his forehead and it only slackened when he resumed whistling again. He was back in the New Estate.

That was not, quite, how it worked out last night. 'Ah no,' she said. He took out the boxes of medals to show them to her and he had the globule with the imprint of the Pope's face on it waiting in his pocket. He suggested that they play a game of strip-poker, and they started to drink the rest of the whiskey.

He kept hinting at what he was getting at, that they should get married. He kept seeing and forgetting that she was topping up his drink. He kept dropping the hint. Do you know what I'm saying to you, do you? And she'd nod. But do you, do you, do you know what I'm saying? And she'd nod. And he gave her the globule. For the moment, he said, let that be a token instead of a ring.

'Ah no.'

Then he lost the head. He hit her. And because he hit her the first time, he hit her the second time. She fell back, got up, there was blood on her mouth. He called her for all the whores that ever lived.

'I'm married!' she said. She was lying. She was crying, she was frightened of him.

He told her to get out, called her for all the whores, to fuck off, yet he kept blocking the door, fucking the medals at her. She was trying to dress and to watch him at the same time and he was coming for her again and she had no place to run, unless she got up on the bed. Then he saw her glance at the table to get one of the bottles there and he went for the table and cleared it, but that was what she wanted him to do because the next thing he saw was the tongs or a leg of a chair coming down on his head.

And he's sorry now. What else can he say? Vera was gone forever for him, Lar's was gone forever. Man had lost the head again and he was paying for it. *Crime and Punishment* by Your Man.

He was still whistling, vigorously, the same tuneless phrase of music as he turned into Blessed Oliver Plunkett Terrace, the street where he lived and, 'Fuck me!' there was someone else coming away from his house. It was too late to duck back. The Greek had seen him too.

The Greek looked like something out of the pictures. He was wearing an old-fashioned suit, probably his grandfather's, because The Greek was a good three or four inches taller than his father. A sort of black frock-coat that was turning green and a waistcoat that looked like faded wallpaper out of a restaurant. He was known to dress up when he was going on a tear. He was carrying a black hat and a cane in the other hand with a silver top.

'How are you, Finbar!'

'I'm not too bad at all, Henry, how's yourself!'

'I hear tell you are chambering with wenches.'

'What, hah? Oh, that!'

'Stable your hounds and we'll go for a drink, the three of us.'

'She's gone back,' said Finbar. 'You're not the first to come looking for her today.'

The Greek frowned, head askew, eying Finbar. 'Are you telling me you have lost your lodger?'

'On me oath! She left early this morning.'

The Greek fixed on Finbar again, considering to himself what Finbar had just said. Then, he said, 'Then you and I together will have a drink. We'll start with a few in Dolly Doran's. Hasten with the beasts, delay defeats equities!'

'I don't mind,' said Finbar, though a drink was the last thing in the world that he wanted. He could not tell The Greek that he was already half-poisoned with alcohol and that only a few moments ago he had been thinking of giving it up altogether because that would be letting The Greek know for certain that Finbar had been riding the sister-in-law. He threaded the dogs along a path through the wares in his garden and went into the house.

The Greek waited, leaning his back against the railings, observing the grey houses on the other side of the street. It did not make sense that Vera had gone back. Not twenty minutes ago he had seen her now famous car still left parked in Elm Park. Equity aids the vigilant.

X

HANGOVER SQUARE

Where was she, oh where was she? What pool or lake or was it the sea?

She had come up for another badly needed gulp of air and the surface that had broken was still shattering like glass on steel about her head. She was a long way out because the voices came from far off and motor-boats, moving short distances, came as muffled sounds through a fog. Were they looking for someone, maybe looking for herself? She had thought of killing herself, what with the way she found decisions difficult, but she had changed her mind.

But where was she?

Vera knew very well where she was. She was sitting in the darkened lobby of the hotel with her handbag in her lap. It is true that she was nodding but it could not be called sleep. A family-size hangover was stalking her. She had to tread carefully. There were times, she found, when it was preferable to submit to the terrors of her imagination, to encourage them to punish her, than to face the reality of her situation.

Splash! It was the sea. And head over heels, like a fish, she went down again. The discovery of what a terrific swimmer she was was mildly surprising. 'She hiver-hovers,' said Mother Dominic out in front of the whole class one day in 2nd Year when Vera's heart was broken, 'but if Vera ever sets her mind to do something, firmly, mind you, she will see it through with flying colours.' Mother Dominic was, and would continue to be, always, Vera's favourite nun.

In the silence down under she could feel the pull of the water on her thighs. Flagellar weeds from beneath licked her and left slime on her stomach. One of them twined itself about her ankle but she shook it off and steadied herself again to watch a column of light that shivered in the water up ahead. Ha-ha-ha! It was elusively playful, rocking of its own accord, reducing itself to half-light, disappearing completely, recovering. Then, just as she was reaching out to it, a cloud of something, a shoal of coloured fish, crossing right to left, thwarted her purpose again. But she was determined to see her hand in the light, even if it killed her, and she waited for them to clear, though she was dying for another gulp of air.

Suddenly, and she knew in advance that it was for no good reason, the fish created two flashing arcs, opening upwards and downwards, and were gone. Shriek! A shoal of blind grey-whiskered woodlice was coming in the opposite direction, a million of them at least. So many were they that they looked like an almost solid mass, except for the ones that were buffeting the edges, that is, unable to hold on or get back in, and the strays.

What would she do? Should she hold her ground? Yes, because the worst possible move in a situation like this would be to attempt to get out of it. The slightest turbulence would break up that flow. And they had no eyes.

They were taking forever. Slowly, they crossed the trembling light, obscuring it and absorbing it into themselves until it became indistinguishable from the surrounding murk, except, that is, for the tip, which was like a star, which made it all the more sad. Wherever were they bound for, she wondered.

Something touched her shoulder in the dark. She did not make a move. Well, the slightest arching to round her shoulder. It was the most outlying one and it bobbed against her again, just as she knew it would. Now she could feel the hard serrated edges as it rotated, searching the contour of her back. Still she waited for the perfect moment and, when it came, with the slightest twitch she sent the louse catapulting off the cliff, the tip of her shoulder-blade, to become lost in the nowhere of forever. Phew!

Shriek! One, two, three, four more of them, outlying ones again, were around her fingers, spinning in the eddies and rocking in a swell they were creating of themselves. They did not have a clue.

Shriek! A chunk had broken off the floating mass, it was fragmenting into hundreds of them, thousands, and they were being drawn into the swell and, struggling and colliding with one another, thinking that they had nosed something in her fingers, they were sucking up to them. Some of them were on their backs.

But what was she going to do, because still they drew?

Ever so carefully she closed the gaps between her fingers, easing out the ones that were sheltering in the inter-spaces and, at the same time, ever so carefully, she turned her hand on edge, rocking it so that those on top should slip down the sides. Then, when she reckoned that enough of them had gathered to weight themselves, here goes, said Vera and ever so carefully she slid her hand upwards out of the cluster of lost creatures and in the same fluent movement she brushed the water over them.

She watched them go, being drawn away in the wake of the others, the ones on their backs showing the lighter grey, the almost-white with a touch of pink of the underbellies, and the lines of tiny club-like feet, paddling since birth, seeming to wave bye-bye. It was a very sad occasion but, definitely, phew!

She badly needed a drink.

Footsteps hurried by while others slowed down to think out their next moves. Voices conversed in gibberish or called out morning greetings in a foreign language to confuse her. Engines growled and, further out, carpenters were hammering timbers. There was a clanging of steel barrels and someone was dropping crates of bottles on concrete.

Whoever had drawn the curtains had not joined them properly in the centre and a bar of light, almost from floor to ceiling, rocked in the fugitive shadows of pedestrians, faded to nothing in the passage of tall vehicles and recovered, as now, in pins of sunshine exploding off cars in the Square. The quartz in the stones of the chimney-breast was luminous, the reception desk, she knew, was behind her, the bundle on the coffee table in front of her was her overnight bag. Of all the stupid places to come to!

She listened to the commerce on the Square, hardly daring to breathe. She should not be here.

Her mouth would not close and it was dry as a board. Her jaw was sore, maybe out of joint, and there were swollen tics of blood on her lips, quick to the touch.

What was she going to do?

Vera knew very well what she was going to do. She was going to lock her family out of the hotel and lock herself in. They would have to break the door down.

But straight thinking or straight talking were not part of the town's or the family's culture: they sounded false. And she had, all her life, tried to emulate the family manner in order to become a full member, without success. If this was going to be her final throw in the game of family, the idea, just envisaged, would have to come out of a tortuous mental process.

And, so, she told herself that she would not dream of doing such a thing. A person would need strong feelings of regret and moral outrage to support such a course of action.

And she rolled with jeebies. She told herself that she was asleep, having nightmares. She told herself, I don't want ten thousand

109

pounds for this place, I want fifteen. She told herself that when she left Finbar's, when not a soul was stirring, she had done so with the object of getting to her car and the thought of the hotel, let alone sleeping in her own bed in her own room, was nowhere in her mind. If the car was still left parked in Elm Park, if it had not been towed away or returned to the car-hire people, she was going to drive it to somewhere quiet so that she could go through the contents of her handbag and thereby ascertain the extent of her problems.

The hotel unfolding as she turned into the Square and cleared the soldier's monument quite took her by surprise. Three substantial storeys of it in terra-cotta paint in a cream surround. Seventeen windows if you included the dormers that peeked over the parapet, one more than the Bank, their boast as children. It was not exactly in the pink, but it was not falling down, which was how she had imagined it since Mary Jane's letter about its not standing the winter and Tom's about its being shut down since February. In her mind's eye she had seen it with the windows boarded up and padlocks on the door. Grilles were protecting the glass on the ground floor windows and the curtains were drawn, but that was not so out of the usual. Then, by chance, she remembered the keys that Miss Rooney had given her.

Her bed was gone. So was everything else. The attic rooms were stripped to the floorboards.

From entering, she had straightaway gone up to her room. There was a smell of lime from the chalky dust that was everywhere and plaster that had been raked out of cracks in the walls crumbled under her feet. All that remained were a few rolls of old lino waiting to be jettisoned out the window on a makeshift chute to the backyard. Perhaps that was where Berry had gone, the remnants of a cot-blanket that was as old as when she was sent to live with Mom. Older. Out the window. The box that contained her childhood possessions, her annuals, the *Dandy*, Dainty, a doll.

She watched the dawn, the staggered wet roofs of the houses

on the Mall and the backyards. The bare room numbed her. The only other things that remained were two discoloured jars on the little cast-iron mantelpiece: a mayonnaise bottle and a jam pot. She had put them there for flowers for the Blessed Virgin. The outline of where the picture hung was still there. Bluebells, lilac, forget-me-nots. Someone was impatient to see the attics as more guest rooms, penthouses perhaps.

Forget me not.

An involuntary gulp stuck in her throat. She was not crying, don't be stupid, she did not cry; she only wanted to know what was the matter because she was not a child. She continued motionless, sitting in the darkened lobby.

From the attics she had gone to the kitchen where she thought she might go through her handbag. All that the giant fridge contained was a half-bottle of milk that had turned yellow. The freezer, though, had enough odds and ends of stuff to keep a person going for a week. There were two cups and a saucer in the sink, and she dribbled water past her swollen lips from one of the cups.

Miss Rooney and the staff had left the kitchen sparkling. Vera loved the table. It was fully ten feet long, white deal, timeless to the touch, its ridges and grooves scrubbed and bleached, knots like toffee. She had often scrubbed it as a girl. On closer inspection it had a few new stains at one end, rings from a cup, and there was a saucerful of cigarette butts. Mary Jane.

Vera put the saucer on the draining-board. Marcia smoked too, quite a lot in fact, but Marcia did everything surreptitiously. Tom smoked a few cheroots in the evening, sometimes. It was hard to tell if he enjoyed them. Perhaps he did not know himself. In everything he did he was one or the other, professionally happy or concerned.

And the dump-heap she had emptied from her handbag and spread out on the table was herself. She stepped back from the array to see if she could choose a shape or colour on which she might concentrate her senses. Even bravest hearts must weep at the sight of heaven's embroidered cloth! There was even a plastic bag of seashells. Pharmaceuticals, papers, hardware, software, an arsenal of contraceptive weaponry – none of which she had used – airline tickets to romantic places – where was her wallet?

As if her head had not been bad enough without being panicked by the thought of a missing wallet! It was to search her overnight bag that she had left in the lobby that brought her back to where she was sitting now. The wallet had been in her hand all the time.

The mess of her life still littered the table back there. She still had to go through it. It was dismaying, and she gulped and, again, it caught in her throat. The tears welled up and she became sad. Momentarily. She was watching this. Don't be so stupid! Sad was a game that she played with perverts.

Vera had been in bigger crises than her present one, undergone and survived – come out on top of! – deeper depressions. Who did they think they were dealing with? She could tell them stories. How to feed mercury to a cheap little fucker and kill him? That her plan for that one was not executed was not her fault: the cheap little fucker did not show up for what would have been his funeral party. She would have seen it through. She would still. As a convent girl she had picked up more in class from the nuns than loving chastity above all things. She could tell stories, if she wanted to.

About once or twice a year she became very down and what did she do about it? She said, okay, if this is the way you want it. It took time, just as it was taking time now. Sometimes the depression lasted for an hour, sometimes for a week, but Vera said, look, I couldn't care less. No sadness, sentimentality, how's your poor uncle, and Jesus fell the eleventh time – for God's sake, we're intelligent human beings after all, aren't we? That was what she did. She let everything go to pot and she sat in the middle of the mess in the middle of her apartment. She didn't go out, answer the phone, the doorbell, she didn't eat. That was all. If someone offered a million bucks for a straight old-fashioned ride, she wouldn't accept it. She would not wash herself. Whose business was it? That was all.

Except, if she found anything soft rising in herself, concern, or a desire to cry, for instance, she raised difficulties. She found a channel on TV that showed nothing and she let it have a good old flicker for itself, day and night. She would not open a window. What for? She had all kinds of pills, her Xanadus she called them, but she would not take a single one of them for all the fucking tea in China, the coffee in Brazil. She sat out her depressions with a certain tightness of the jaws. Then, when she started to put her house back in order and wash herself, she knew she had won.

Just give her a little more time with this one. Let her roll a little more with the jeebies.

That was why Finbar's place had appealed to her. At first, that is. The filth. But Finbar's place had not done her any good. I mean to say, she told herself, his place, the smell of it, and his rat, exceeded squalor and filth. How does anyone live like that? His lavatory! Where water – if that was what it was – dripped on your head, ran down your back. Where you had to keep your feet up. And when you put them down you risked stepping on things. Jesus, the crunch they made in the dark! His place was infested with them. Cockroaches in New York? Tawny, almost see-through, fast-moving, evil-looking strings of things that moved precisely. And the woodlice! She had watched them by daylight pursuing grey laborious lives across the floor and, by candle-light, doing pilgrimages up the fucking walls. There were mice behind the skirting-board under the head of that poxy little bed that would cripple you. They had great old scratching times for themselves in there and came out to play in the small hours and left their calling-cards, black droppings, in the sugar bowl. All kinds of rubbish, dog-shit and bones in the back-garden, but, yes, most importantly, there was a rat out there who had given up. How could anyone live like that? The back-garden was a place of dogs, yet the rat wandered the middle of it. The rat had lost interest and defiance, had lost heart, and was only waiting for someone to bring the back of a spade down on its head.

Finbar's had done her no good. Everything was dirt and lies. The only clean and honest thing that happened was the row. It was a good thing that he had hit her and it was a better thing that she had finished the matter by bringing the flat side of the stick of furniture down on his head. Otherwise she would still be there.

Poor Finbar. When she sorted out her affairs she would call on him and say – whatever.

So, what was she going to do?

The hammering on the Square was the worst but it was sporadic and, mercifully to her head, she had not heard it for some time. Whatever it was that they were building out there. A scaffold, ha-ha-ha! Did she have a choice about what she was going to do? She could not leave, not now, not in broad daylight, not in front of that innocent-sounding activity out there, not in the condition she was in. It was not only her mouth. She was filthy, she stank, she could smell herself, for God's sake! A moment ago she felt dizzy, her elbows shook when she thought to rise to get another drink of water. Her back was twisted from fucking in that little bed. She was depressed, she told you that, for God's sake!

She would wait here until dark.

A light flashed jaggedly from the direction of the door, and she thought that she was caught. It was followed immediately by a clacking, like the springing of a trap. It took her a moment to realize that it was the postman.

Yes, what if someone arrives before dark? Please, Jesus, she prayed, let no one arrive, and she got to her feet. Prayers alone would not stop them from showing up if they wanted to, from entering and discovering her. To her sinking heart she admitted that she was thinking of locking the door. Please, Jesus, do not let her lock the door to her brother and sisters. If they turned up and found themselves locked out they would be furious, they would be – Mary Jane's word – mortified at this public offence against the

114

sanctity of the family. Please, Jesus. He was no use to her. Fear drove her on in the dark, one small step at a time, towards the glass-panelled vestibule that surrounded the front door.

Where was all this fear of hers coming from?

Finbar's fear yesterday when the police arrived was nothing compared to hers when Tom called some time later.

'How yeh doin'!' he said, the kind of unexpected thing that is said to you in a dream to frighten you. He had lost his neck, his shoulders were fully up about his ears to disguise himself to the New Estate and, of all things, his face was merry.

'How yeh doin'!'

She heard the tap and thought that it was Finbar who had gone out with the dogs earlier and who had, she thought, in his agitated state, maybe forgotten his keys.

The eager 'o' of Tom's mouth and his merry eyes, the lapel badge, the jacket of his double-breasted suit that she never saw unbuttoned on him, only just containing him, 'How yeh doin'!' and she slammed the door in the terror of finding him there. She heard him sucking in air outside.

'Vera?'

But she held her breath, flattened her back against the wall and would not budge, she did not dare, until he went away.

Busy, happy-sounding pedestrians were inches from her ear. There were letters on the mat under her feet. Her fingers had found the locks and they were waiting for the perfect moment to activate the double-bolts. In the meantime she was conjuring up pictures of her family, ones that would, hopefully, at this late stage, dissuade her. Please.

She never met anyone with a temper like Mary Jane's. The world was meant to go Mary Jane's way and when it didn't she despised the world and everything in it, including herself. She warned herself, her fists inches from her face. Then she pursued her fists, spitting at them. The intensity of her rage turned her white and gave her a starved look and it was all the more terrible because she did not quite know how to let go. Her eyes turned white and they burned the room, scanning it slowly for something to break, the cheapest. But every other object had felt threatened. She ran little steps to get away from herself, she would not scream, she shook. Then she broke down in a kind of laughter and tears. Still, it was better to keep away from her. To compliment or sympathize – in either form – brought on a new and worse bout, now with the sympathizer as the target of her venom and receiving perhaps, in conclusion, a backwards thump from her white knuckles before she walked off, sawing the air with her elbow, laughing bitterly at the ceiling and snapping her fingers at it. Declan was very frightened of her and she despised him for it.

But she was not the worst. Vera was sorry for Mary Jane. Marcia was the worst. She was so fucking dumb. Marcia, Vera believed, would still pinch you. Mary Jane was frightened of Marcia's teeth! Poeple like Marcia do not change. Marcia, a woman with six children, Vera's sister, would slowly Indian-burn your wrist, twist your arm or pinch you pitilessly while chewing a cud of sweets.

And why was Vera thinking of Joan of Arc? Tom. Tom's word, flaming. Flaming: the stake.

The door vibrated in the passage of a heavy truck. It was the perfect moment and, here goes, said Vera. She pressed the buttons upwards, simultaneously, on the two locks and the double-bolts shot home to their keepers. They shot into her heart, too, stopping it.

But in the next moment it was pounding with excitement. She was back in the lobby, making her way along a wall. The back door too had to be secured. She heard her breath laughing at the dark. She handed the emptiness across the opening that led to the lounge bar and found the wall again. Some tightrope walking this for a woman who wants just one pound to make twelve stone! This was becoming heady stuff for Vera. Her toe probed for the next obstacle, the steps that turned from the stairs into the lobby. And after the steps there would be the

pillar at the top of the passageway. She was doing famous-
ly.

Down the passageway, at the turn, a dim light fell on a patch
of carpet. It came, she knew, through the lace on the dining-room
door. Why had she stopped when she could proceed with greater
confidence now? Something was about to happen.

A half-swoon washed over her. She found the pillar and held
on to it. The moment passed, or so it seemed. She did not trust it.
Devil hangover. If it did not get you one way, it tried another. Her
headache, she realized now, had disappeared some time ago: she
should have been more alert to the warning that the jeebies had
gone elsewhere to attack her from a new direction. She waited,
listening for a move from them.

What was she doing? She stepped out of herself for a moment,
to watch herself standing there, leaning against a pillar with her
handbag in her hand, in the near dark, afraid to make a sound,
afraid to put on a light in a place they called home. She would be
thirty-eight years of age tomorrow. Was she going crazy?

The boards creaked above her. Silence again. She listened as if
to hear her mother's voice, the thump of her mother's body against
bedroom doors as she roamed the corridors. She remembered Uncle
Willie – she saw him – looking at his glass eye in the mirror, then in
the barrel of water. She thought of her father. The very notion of
gaiety irritated him. It made him close his lips. His presence in this
moment was standing close behind her. She did not look back or
move because she knew he would not touch her. There was never
a whisper, in the line of insanity, about her father, but Vera had
often watched him secretly and wondered how such gravity was
possible.

She took a step along the passageway. The idea of getting to
the kitchen to secure the back door was beginning to seem like
a very long journey. A second step. Another half-swoon overtook
her and was gone. She pressed her face to the wall and waited
to see what it would do next, and to resist it if she could. On

second thoughts, two steps sidewards to return to the pillar. She was nobody's fool.

The nausea rose up inside her again and gathered in her throat. The place was becoming airless, her knees were weak, she felt the hot sweat begin. She embraced the pillar and rolled her forehead on its cold surface. 'There's gotta be something better than this.'

The sickness came again, now wave was following wave, and she rotated her body into the corner created by the pillar and the wall and wedged herself there. 'There's gotta be something better than this.' Deep folds overlapped and overran themselves in front of her eyes, creating moments of total darkness and flashes of light. She pressed her shoulders and her head harder into the corner. She did not want to go down. Her handbag, empty as it was, weighed a ton but she would not release it. She-would-not-release-it, no matter what. Her hair, pressed against the concrete, felt like ropes: she surely looked a mess. But she was nobody's pushover.

Her back slid down the wall and she sat on her legs in the corner. She was burning. If it be possible let this chalice pass from me. Moans of laughter ran the length of the passageway and returned, bouncing off the walls, in answer to her prayer. A sound to put the heart crossways in mice. The disembodied voice, she realized, was her own and she cast it again, and again, into the cavern of the passageway and got on to her hands and knees.

Come on then, old devil, fucker, sickness, do your fucking best! Screw me, fuck me, rook me if you are able!

Stiff-armed, she was swaying over her hands and knees, and she began to laugh harshly at the innocent astonishment of her eyes.

All she had wanted to do was give this airless place to them!

Her hair brushed the carpet, her mouth was open, hopeful of a draught of air across the floor. Cramps were tightening her stomach and she lay on it, drew her handbag under her that the increased pressure might relieve the pain. Must filled her nose and mouth, her fingers scraped at scabs of hardened gum.

'How yeh doin'!'

Curled around her handbag, she laughed, rolling from side to side to find the position that would relieve the pain. Now, rolling again, she was trying to get up, and failing. And did Mom laugh too in her attempts to get up off the concrete floor after crawling out of the fire?

Vera got to her hands and knees, braced herself, hands spanned, touching the floor and the wall with the tips of her fingers, and in one fierce effort she got to her feet. Come on then, devil, sickness, madness, fuckers, friends and kind relations, kill me if you can, but don't any one of you fucking-well insult me!

The outline of the door facing her was the door to the gents and she thrust her body against it. Inside, her hands searched the pitch black. Her sleeve brushed something and it flew from her, clattering and flapping. She turned, swinging her bag to establish the sides of the cubicle and dropped to her knees. She clung to the bowl, trying to vomit. If she could puke she would have the fucker. The fucker would not yield. It wanted her unconscious and, as always, even with sleep, the moments of going into that vast colourless place frightened her. Maybe she should go out to them and surrender on the Square.

Unearthly moans reverberated above her. The tiles beneath were freezing. Her forehead was turning to marble, ice-cold as death. It was growing silent. It was becoming grey all over. The handbag was slipping through her fingers.

All the doors were closed and shuttered, all the radial streets were bare. She was circling the Square in the careful steps of a dancer. It was mildly puzzling. Other than Harry St John, who was standing by the monument, there was nobody else about. Other than that old round woman sitting on the ridge-tiles of O'Connor's roof, that is. The boots, the black satinette with the metallic sheen, the shawl tucked under her arms in front. Vera had her suspicions as to who the old round woman was but, rather than stepping back to gawk up again, she would continue her circle and establish the matter more cleverly when she got back to the hotel side again.

119

Then she noticed that Harry St John was carrying a newspaper, was tapping it nervously on the side of his knee and she knew what was up. Everybody in the town was at the funeral of course.

'Soul of my Saviour, sanctify my . . . of my Saviour . . . body of Christ be . . . deep in thy wounds, Lord . . . so-o shall I . . . hide and shelter me . . . So-o shall I never . . . part from thee.'

A mile of mourning voices followed the body of Christ. The funeral was going up St Kevin's Hill, she reckoned, and it stretched back as far as St Malachy's Grove. A breeze bent the hymn and took pieces out of it. Now it was turning into St Columba's Avenue.

'O bleh heh Jee hee!' Father O'Loughlin's ungovernable voice crackled in the loudspeaker and sounded cross, exhorting them to rise it and to sing in unison but, 'So-o shall I never': there were too many of them and they were too sad to do so of course, they did not know what street the body would lead them into next because it could go anywhere it liked, they were starving and the pace was only fit for the short legs of the infants. But it would all end in Benediction on the Square. That was what the platform that they had erected was doing there. And Harry St John was waiting for them, to protest with his newspaper, the *News of the World*, and Mom was in bad humour on O'Connor's roof. Vera was in bad company.

'Who cares?' said Vera. 'For God's sake!'

Because the worst thing in the world in a situation like this was to show that you were frightened, and she began to dance.

For instance, last time on the scales she weighed one hundred and sixty-seven pounds, that is, eleven stone thirteen, so her lightness of step was mildly surprising. Still, a woman without an arse is no good. And, when you thought about it, she was five feet ten and a half without her shoes on, and men liked it. She could spin like a top. There. And she never had any particular interest in this kind of dancing which was classical. On the contrary, because even in those far-off days when everyone knew that they were going to be an air hostess, a nun, a bank clerk, a radiologist or a poultry

120

instructress, and Vera didn't, and it was suggested in class one day by Sally Downey that she might try her hand at the dancing, joking her of course, Vera just shrugged one shoulder, like so. Leap, alight, turn, glide, hop, skip, jump. It just goes to show how wrong people can be, how wrong one can be about oneself, n'est-ce pas?

Back in those days when Vera was a beanpole, don't ask her how, when Sally or someone suggested a model maybe, joking her again of course, Vera never dreamt of such a thing and did her Charlie Chaplin walk for them. Still, she must have dreamt a little about it because when Wally the Swede, her boyfriend, put the very same suggestion to her in a bar on 44th and 8th, though she had filled out on top and more on bottom at the time, not to mention her waist, she went with him to Vincenzo's Salon to take off her clothes, try her hand at the game, to walk the plank, to call herself Kathleen. Money for jam for the two of them.

So strong was his thirst to receive her faith that he kindled within her the fire of love. She loved Wally the Swede, body and soul, she loved everything about him, she would do anything for him. His jaws were like the mould-boards of a plough and they made her laugh. Laugh. The afternoons in bed, where everything made sense, every part of her, until her feet touched the floor again. O heart for me on fire, strengthen me with passion, hide in me, deeper in my wounds, be thou my saving guest, shelter me, bathe me in thy tide. And after it, the serious part, the ecstasy, they laughed until they were helpless at their own earnestness. Because there is nothing more earnest than sex. So-o shall I never, never part from thee. They said that he had fallen but she knew he had been pushed from the window by a cheap little fucker. Heigh-ho. She would love him forever.

It was Mom up there, all right, in all her roundness on the roof, the heel of her fist propping her chin, thinking things out. Typical. Preoccupied as she was with her own problems, she did not miss much. Vera so wanted a sign from Mom. Mom, she knew, was thinking whether or not to go next or near the Imperial Hotel at all, to see her own strap of a daughter and her little baldy small O'Toole man and, if she did, were her shawl and her boots not good enough to enter by the front door? It was hard to please the jolter-headed gawpsheets living in this cursed place, the town, where they would build a nest in your ear. She did not like them. Vera saw her draw a deep breath and hold it. Vera did the same and waited, hopefully. Then, and still without ever looking at Vera, Mom touched her bun and nodded the once in the slow formal manner her approval of the dance and to continue, child. And Vera was so grateful.

The ground was alive from the sun and fine sand and wisps of straw rolled under the soles of her feet, producing delightful sensations, and, if they adhered, at her most idle manoeuvre they fell away again, silver and gold descending. Mom was beginning to look interested. Vera bent her knees and jumped into the air, and again, spiralling this time. Mom was delighted, her hands held out were pressed together. And, for her next trick, Vera hovered between the worlds before descending. Mom threw back her head in laughter. And for her next trick, Vera began to run. The warm air became a summer breeze, fanning out her hair as she took striding leaps with her arms and legs so wide apart they were horizontal to the ground, to elegantly descend each time, to race again, to what to do next, to spin like a top, to pirouette, yes. Oh, freedom, heaven, oh, exhilaration!

Oh! What? The funeral procession was coming round the corner into the Mall and Vera was barefoot, yes, okay, but was she dressed? Fortunately, she was spinning like a top and, fortunately, her chin was resting on her collar-bone, the way all good dancers do it so that they can check such matters out. Her white dress was like a juggler's plate rotating between two spindles. Phew!

'Sweet Heart of Jesus, font of love and mercy, today we come, thy blessing to implore.'

The acoustics of the Mall were perfect and the singing now was lusty because the end was in sight. A river of heads was streaming up the Mall. The tips of the four spears that supported the canopy at the head of the procession were emerging out of a dip. Though Vera was dressed, she felt that she should not be here, that she should get to hell out of it. Now she could see the monstrance that contained the body under the canopy.

Shriek! The sun caught it and it grinned back impishly like a wall-eyed sunflower bent on mischief.

Aargh! Tom was carrying it. He was wall-eyed also in the excitement of being given such an honour and was only just containing himself from breaking into a run. The closest relatives followed, the bishop dressed in red and the others in white surplices. Then came the dignitaries and the merchants of the town, some of them in sashes. At any moment now, the seven thousand sympathizers that followed would break ranks, overtake the body and rush the Square to get good places. Some of them had bicycles for the purpose.

What was Vera going to do? She needed a friend. Poised on the balls of her feet to run or to stay, she glanced up at the roof. Mom was gone. There was only a patch of wet where Mom had sat, some hair-pins and red dust. There was no one to advise her. A sense of delighted terror held her there. And Harry St John had unrolled the *News of the World*, was pretending to read it, holding it up prominently before his face. The procession was almost on the Square.

'Font of love!' Someone shouted, laughing raucously. 'Font of love!' Who was shouting? Shriek, rarp, erk, eek, aargh! Vera was dancing a jig, facing the mouth of the Mall, her white dress lifted as far as it would go: 'Font of love!'

When she came to she thought that she was dead. The silence. The blackness. Where was she? She felt completely humbled. Then she became aware of a sound like castanets. Was she dreaming? Her teeth were chattering, she was drenched in a cold sweat.

She hauled herself up, sat on the bowl and leaned over. Give her a few minutes. Apart from a cold ball of pain inside her forehead, the sickness was gone, but, Jesus, there's gotta be something better

123

than this. Her condition was hardly a matter for congratulations. She felt like a scabby-headed ape in a cave the way her arms were hanging down from her. And the sickness would be back. She was sure of it. Where was she going to find the strength to deal with it? Yes; maybe, after all, she should go out to them and let them put her down.

Heigh-ho! It was time to see to the back door.

Something wraith-like, crimson and purple, drifted past her and was sucked up into the turn of the stairs. She had paused in the passageway to adjust to the new shifting light. The ghost of her mother was having a busy day of it. Vera went off in the other direction. Definitely, there was a whole lot of insanity in this O'Toole family but it did not include her.

She went through the cheerless light of the dining-room without stopping. One whole wall, floor to ceiling, was in glass but it looked out on the covered porchway that led from the Square to the yard. Stripped of linen, the tables looked cheap. She had often laid those tables, done a lot of work around the place, more than the chores that were set her, very much more than Mary Jane. It was not that she was fond of work; it was in the hope, really, of getting her father's and mother's attention. Marcia was deliberately pathetic so that they would give up on her doing anything. Tom was required to study. He polished his shoes.

Full daylight streamed into the kitchen. The back door was secure. Two bolts, two locks and the old-fashioned latch.

Why was she frowning? Her brows had come down of themselves, her eyes were screwed up under them. It passed.

The contents of her handbag strewn on the table: all it needed, she thought, was seagulls. She selected a card of pills and took them to the sink. It was a nigh-hopeless measure taking a pill at this stage and more than likely it would bring on the nausea again. The memory of her feet up in stirrups decided the matter. Take two, she told herself, try three.

Why was she looking like a dog again?

Stiff-armed, to support herself, she was holding the sink and gagging over it. Her knees were shaking and she was hot again. Bells were ringing in her head. Third and final round. Okay.

But, this time, if she was not going to faint, she needed air. The back door was like Fort Knox, it would take too long to open it. On tiptoes, she reached over the sink for the handle of the iron window. It would not budge. She hauled a resistant chair from the table, its legs hopping and screeching over the tiles, and set it on the duck-board by the sink. It wobbled and fell over backwards as she climbed on to the draining-board. My, this big whore was living dangerously! Her father's presence came into the kitchen behind her. Good! She dressed the presence in blue serge, a three-piece, put a fob watch in the cup of his hand so that he could time her.

'Go!' He mouthed the word, silently, frowning down at his watch.

Thump! The handle went up and she pushed the window open. The saucerful of Mary Jane's butts was under her and she swept it into the sink where she heard it shattering. In slow motion her hands took the next obstacle, jumping the taps, and came down in the recess, scattering glass jars of powder to the left and right out of their way. Her head was over the yard. Her body wanted to collapse but she refused. On hands and knees was how she wanted it. Her body wanted to convulse but she was not having any of that either. Heave, yes, sway, yes, in regular motion. She was in control of this exorcism.

Swoosh! And the devil came forth from her mouth, arcing upwards in attempted flight, but to no avail, and fell to a colourful death on the earth below where he belonged. Splat! And all his works and pomps were with him.

The earth below, she noticed, was a new concrete path. It still had a timber batten, sunk in the cobblestones, encasing the outside. And Vera was pleased. She wiped her mouth and gave a final spit. Satan, get thee fucking gone!

125

What did Daddy think of the yield? Daddy, too, was gone so he must not have been impressed.

It was strange to see the yard so quiet. The doors on the line of sheds, stabling for horses from the old days, were closed. On the cobblestones in the centre was the remains of a fire. The funeral pyre of Dainty, her doll, Berry, her blanket? She kicked off her shoes behind her. It was a pity that her hair was so matted with dirt because it would be lovely to feel the soft air move through it.

No one would show up today.

Her eyelids were so heavy they were making her smile, and she lowered her body sideways to rest her head on her arm. Just for the few minutes. The other arm hung over her head into the yard, giving a pleasant stretch to her back. The Angelus tolled in the sunshine, eighteen bells for the dead. And at this remove the sounds of the Square came as the drone of satisfied insects.

It appeared to Vera that she was hanging out of the kitchen window of the Imperial Hotel, stuck there, and there was a red-haired youth in one of the sheds, whistling to himself and changing into a white boiler suit. Could that be so or was she dreaming? She had heard, she thought, what sounded like the pedal of a bicycle catch in the small door that was cut in the large porch doors, hollow coughs and footsteps in the porchway. Then this nicely turned-out youth, who was changing in the shed, crossed the yard, reading the instructions on a yellow box that looked to her like Polyfilla. He had snorted loudly and spat in a manner that was out of keeping with his ginger curls, in the manner of someone who believes himself to be unobserved.

He was coming out into the sunshine now, weighing the merits of two old pans that he had found. He threw one of the pans back into the shed and commenced to wipe cobwebs and blow dust off the other one. He was about to see her.

The discovery of a battered-looking woman, hanging out of a window over a pool of vomit, will stand to him in later years, she thought, stirring herself to twist herself free of the taps and the cheek of the window's recess. Her movements would let him know she was not dead and, in further consideration of him, she kept her eyes down so as not to add embarrassment to the first moments of his shock.

He was crouched, fiercely concentrated on her, ready to spring, a tennis player with a frying-pan.

She shrugged from the hands and knees position, that's life.

The situation, both sides, she knew, would look funny to an objective observer and, indeed, for a moment she thought that she was going to laugh. The next moment was strange. She did not know the boy but, obviously, he was from the town, her hometown. An innocent longing had overtaken her. How lovely it would be to sit out there in the sunshine with the boy and idly chat. Just for a few minutes.

'How yeh!' said Vera in the accent of the town.

'Get out!' His voice cracked.

Now that he had spoken, his feet became unstuck and he swayed in half-lunges, the pan raised threateningly.

No. She smiled to reassure him and to explain. 'Lovely morning!'

'Get out!' His voice had deepened. There was disgust on his face. 'What're you doin' here! Get out, you dirty tramp! Clear!'

'It's okay,' said Vera, 'I'm the owner.'

Had she heard what she had just said it would have surprised her.

'Right,' he said. 'I'm going down for the Guards.'

He was removing his boiler suit with unnecessary violence. He was not listening either or, if he was, the equation of ownership and Vera's appearance did not make sense. Not yet, at any rate.

She arsed her way back into the kitchen, watching him. His wild-eyed declaration to have her hunted had begun to question itself. He stepped out of the boiler suit in the shed doorway. His eyes had grown suspicious of himself, of his first reading of the situation.

'It's not morning,' he said, correcting her. The tone was not conversational but neither was he being abusive of her any more.

He was advising himself that it might be rash, unwise, to hand a matter over to the Guards when it possibly held greater advantage to himself, handled in a different way. The darkness swallowed the calculation on his face as he stepped back into the shed.

Vera picked up the overturned chair, carried it to the table and stood there, absently, forgetting to put it down. She had hurt her shin and then her hip, climbing down off the draining-board. But that was not what was annoying her. 'This is my chair.' She mouthed the words to herself without knowing what her object was in saying them.

The boy had returned to the yard. She could hear him shuffling and coughing politely to attract her attention. She preferred the spontaneity that had animated his anger and cracked his voice earlier: it was a natural thing. What age was he? Sixteen? She hesitated over returning to the window. It would be unfair to start insulting the boy. But she wanted to close that window.

The pan now might be a cap the way he carried it by its rim. At her reappearance in the window he looked up at the sky to admire the day that was in it. She nodded to him, her face impassive, to go on with the ritual.

'Isn't it a grand day, ma'am, after all that last night's rain?'

'Are you young or are you old?' said Vera.

'What, ma'am?'

Vera shook her head: it did not matter.

He placed the pan, face down, in front of him on the cobble-stones. He straightened up again and began to draw upon the back of the pan with his toe to show the awkwardness and the innocence of youth.

'I'm working for Mr O'Toole,' he said, 'preparing the attics for him, like.'

Vera set the chair for herself and climbed on to the draining-board again. When he saw that her purpose was to shut the window, he started forward to come to her assistance.

She shook her head, stopping him. She reached out for the

handle and, again, he was coming forward eagerly. She shook her head vigorously, 'No,' forming the word by pushing out her lips excessively so that he would see the better what he had seen before, the purple bruises on her mouth. And – she pointed at them – what about her hair, what about the pool of puke? He nodded wise understanding.

Vera started laughing. At first she was laughing at her own actions but when he grinned back, catering for her, she pointed at him: she was laughing at him. He looked down to see what was wrong. She kept pointing and laughing.

He was becoming cross. He wanted to kick something. Good: she nodded encouragement. But he started to grow old with wisdom again.

'Or would you prefer to take a punch at this, Sunshine?' She lifted her skirt.

Now, definitely, he was young, a male child. What the sight of a woman's thighs or breasts can do to them! She regarded him for a moment to show her authority: 'Yes?' Then she winked to herself in the shrewd manner of the town to let him know she had his measure.

She closed the window.

Now he was a slow hammer-thrower, turning a circle. He had returned to his pan and picked it up. But if he let it fly it might break something in one of the yards on either side. He glanced at her again and she smiled back and nodded. He pitched the pan high into the air and then he had to run out of the way of its crazy descent.

His bike rattled the porch doors. He was gone. Momentarily she regretted her cruelty but then she said, 'Fuck him!' It was unlikely that he would go home and simply have a wank for himself, he would be reporting her occupation of the hotel. Good! 'And fuck them too!'

Why was she opening the back door?

Halfway along the porchway the small door in the porch doors swung open and a local in a cap was stooped outside, looking in. The truncated body of the boy was telling the local: 'Put the shit crossways in me! Fuckin' mad!' The man in the cap ducked back smartly at the sight of Vera.

'Jasus tonight!' The boy was jumping on his bicycle as Vera slammed the door shut. Then she bolted it.

She locked and bolted the kitchen door again. And what did she have to do next? She sat down but was up again in a moment. She was unable to stay in one place. She put her shampoo, cigarettes and lighter to one side and began to sweep the other objects on the table back into her handbag. She did not have to go through all this shit to assess her situation. She knew what was important. She had a good idea of what was left in her wallet. The return part of her New York–Dublin ticket was blown: that was for last Wednesday morning. The other ticket, New York–Atlanta, was for today. Some hope, Atlanta, now! She had borrowed the money to come home on the strength of the Atlanta job and booked the two tickets at the same time in case she spent the money: ha-ha! The consequences of her not being in Atlanta for the weekend-long party could have her laughing to death. Those people would dump you in the river, carve you up or throw you out a window. She had trouble on both sides of the Atlantic.

She collected her overnight bag and went upstairs.

The Parnell Room was blessed and rechristened The Marian Suite in 1954. It overlooked the Square, it had a four-poster bed and was the only room in the hotel with a bath of its own. As children they used to dare one another to dash in and out of it. Uncle Brendan, when he came to live with the family, lasted only two nights in it. It was too grand for him entirely, he said. It was said to be haunted by a pale woman in a long brown dress who sat in the painted armchair, weeping continuously. From the corridor, Vera tossed her overnight bag unceremoniously in the door and went off for towels and bed linen and to switch on the heating for the water. And perhaps there were some clothes of her mother's that she could borrow.

She undressed and got into her dressing-gown. Her suede suit would never recover.

While the water heated, she sat on one side of one of the bedroom windows, where she could not be seen, watching the Square.

The Square filled up with cars and people every day and emptied itself bare at night; a bit of a mystery because what, really, was going on? It was full now. Delivery vans blocked good-natured traffic, smart-footed men looked purposeful and went into Lynch's the newsagent, came out, tapping paper batons in their hands, to pause, to wonder where they had to go next. There was something submissive about the women shoppers in the way that they appeared to shuffle piously. Two men were erecting or dismantling a platform: it was hard to tell which. A mystery. And the scene, for all its seeming casualness, was comprised of people who were watchful and judgemental of the most ordinary things. The man in the cap who had peered in the porchway at her looked casual too in his new position across the Square outside O'Connor's.

She washed her hair, brushed her teeth and had a bath. After drying herself she got into her mother's nightdress, switched on the electric fire that stood in front of the grate, and the bedside lamp. Then she went to the bedroom window and stood fully in front of it.

All her life she had wanted to do something in her hometown without being judged. Without caring whether she was judged or not. To find the bottom of the town, you know, if it had one, where people did things without the advice or consent of anyone. It was not that she had ever wished her father and mother dead, but she used to think that when they passed on, when it would no longer matter to them or embarrass them, she would engage her curiosity about the town in one right crazy rave-up of a party.

The phone was ringing downstairs.

The man in the cap outside O'Connor's had a companion at this stage and they were watching her. Good. With slow deliberation, ceremoniously, she drew the drapes together, then she did similarly to the other bedroom window.

She got into bed and lit a cigarette. A cup of tea would be nice but she was not going to bother about it now. She was comfortable. She would have something to eat later on. Her mouth would be okay again tomorrow. Lips were fast healers. It would have been a worse situation had it been a black eye. The phone was ringing in the room next door, the sitting-room. It would take them several hours, she reckoned, to decide to break down the door.

She extinguished the cigarette and switched off the light. The electric fire gave a warm glow to the room. She fixed her eyes on the painted armchair, the one that the ghost of the weeping woman occupied.

The front doorbell joined in with the telephones.

All her life the feeling of belonging had eluded her and there was no reason to imagine that she would find it now. And, oh yes, she had prayed for the grace that would conform her, make her worthy of her family. But was being worthy of her family such a big deal, so desirable a thing? Fearful as it was to say so, no.

She was disappearing out of herself, even from her face, into sleep, the vast colourless place. Awesome. An astronaut again, like the one in the movie where the umbilical cord is severed and he floats off into space and is left out there forever. She could rescue herself by touching something cold or by placing her hands, palms downwards, on the bed. She was frightened but, this time, she was determined and she went with the sensation, willingly, to discover the living depth of isolation because, whatever else about it, it was clean.

'Cheer up!' she said to the ghost of the weeping woman. 'Oh well,' she said then, turning on to her other side, 'if you're determined to be miserable about it!'

She knew exactly where she was. She was waking up in The

Marian Suite of the Imperial Hotel. She thought that they would have shouldered in or broken down the front door, in the way that the Conneeleys had broken into Mom's house, but the sound she was hearing was a ladder, scraping and being jumped across the wall outside to a window of her room. The ladder was bowing now and creaking under the weight of a man. Tom?

Should she switch on a light before a window was broken? There was probably a crowd down there, watching. They deserved to see a window being broken. She got out of bed, quietly, put on her dressing-gown and waited.

A pane of glass shattered and fell behind the drapes. 'Who the fuck's damaging my property?' was what she had decided to say, but the words did not come. A second pane came in. There was a sharp intake of breath from outside. He was having difficulty in getting at the latch.

'What is going on?' said Vera.

She switched on the lights and took up a book to present herself as a woman who was going about her normal business before being disturbed.

There was no reply from outside and she drew back the drapes. Of course it was not Tom. It was the younger of the two policemen who had called to Finbar's yesterday, apparently to establish that she was alive. From the blankness of his face, it would appear that now he had expected to find her in a coma, at the least.

It was night on the Square. The blue light of the police car was flashing, there was an ambulance waiting and a crowd had gathered.

'What is this?' said Vera.

The Garda shook his head, nothing. Then he looked down at the Square for a better answer to her question.

'We were requested to – ' he said. 'There was speculation that you might have . . .' He left it unfinished.

'Look at the goddamn window!' said Vera, gesturing at it with the book. A show of annoyance that was visible to the

133

assembly on the Square. 'What's all this about? I ask a simple question!'

The young policeman was fed up. And his hand was bleeding. 'You didn't answer the phone or the door,' he said.

'It's the custom to break people's windows when they do not answer the phone?'

No. He shook his head.

'Do you require anything else?'

No. He contained a sigh and began his descent.

'Hello!' said Vera. Then, in a clear voice she called out, 'My property!'

She considered drawing the drapes together again and decided against it. Instead, she drew back the drapes of the other window. What had she to do next? Wait for them to make their next move. She went to the window of the unlit bathroom to watch the scene breaking up on the Square. If Tom, Mary Jane and Marcia were down there, they were keeping out of sight. But they would show up of course. In the meantime there were all kinds of things in the freezer downstairs. And she felt like a glass of champagne.

1.00 a.m. Not that she would have let them in, but no one showed up. Intermittently, she had moved from bedroom to bathroom to watch the Square become deserted. Last time she looked, there was only a small brown terrier down there, sleeping in Lynch's doorway. The last straggler, coming from somewhere, had crossed the Square half an hour ago and gone homewards, unaware of her existence. The occasional car passing by at speed was all she could hear now. It was disappointing.

She had brought a tray of drinks upstairs because she wanted to treat herself. The blue cotton dress of her mother's suited her and she had put a ribbon in her hair.

The footsteps of another straggler came into the Square and she listened, waiting for them to pass by.

'Vera!'

134

The voice came from out on the Square and in the next moment the doorbell rang. There were two of them in it.

'Vera!'

She went to the bathroom window.

'We have come unarmed and alone!'

The Greek was on the Square. Someone else was giggling, pressing the doorbell. The Greek was sweeping the ground with a large black hat, like an actor, and holding up a silver-topped cane in the other hand.

'Let down the bridge, we pray you in the name of the Most High!'

The birthday girl laughed and skipped down the stairs.

XI

THERE IS NOTHING SO FUTILE
AS PLANNING FOR PLEASURE

(i)

'I have nothing to declare but my schizophrenia,' said The Greek.

'Come in,' said Vera.

'You are very good,' said The Greek.

Finbar held back on the footpath outside the door. He had not counted on seeing Vera so fresh and respectable-looking. He grew small – this time his shrinking was deliberate – and he grimaced painfully to himself. This was a demonstration of contrition for the night before which, until he saw her in the blue dress and with a yellow ribbon in her hair, he thought would not be necessary.

'Come in.'

He had a quick look up and down and slipped past her into the hotel.

'In the sitting-room you would have us?' said The Greek, already on his way up the stairs.

Finbar waited at the foot of the stairs to let Vera go ahead of him and she acknowledged the gesture with a smile. She would, though, have to control her amusement of The Greek before facing him again. His get-up and manner reminded her of New York friends who called sometimes on Sunday afternoons. And he was, possibly, the man she was looking for.

'Good Lord!' said The Greek, stopped in the sitting-room doorway.

The sitting-room, the traditional place in the hotel for after-hours drinking for non-residents, was chock-a-block with files of the hotel's accounts and ledgers. It looked like somebody's temporary office. There were sheets of architects' drawings pinned on a wall and others on the floor, plans of the different areas of the hotel.

'We can go in here,' said Vera.

The Greek's assumed authoritativeness betrayed itself in momentary surprise at the suggestion of drinking in a bedroom with a woman at this early stage. But then, going into The Marian Suite, he said, 'Ah, good old Charles's place!'

'Whose?' said Finbar, now following close The Greek's heels.

'Charles Stewart Parnell,' said The Greek. 'He slept a night here once, God love'm!'

Vera drew the drapes together and Finbar saw The Greek noting the softness of the backs of her legs. She was wearing no stockings. He began to sit down but as The Greek was still standing he rose again.

'Sit down,' said Vera to him.

Finbar put his hands in his overcoat pockets and sat in the painted armchair. 'The Guards,' he said.

'Hmm?' said Vera, and opened her hands wide to ask them what they would like.

'The Guards have raided every hostelry in town tonight,' said The Greek, 'including Mannions – an unheard-of precedent in

137

modern times. Stephen Mannion knows that I can handle them, and he obliged us with a few in the kitchen, but then he cracked under the pressure of Julia's walking-stick on the ceiling above our heads.'

'They're after promotion, all right,' said Finbar.

'What would you like?' said Vera, laughing.

'What would you like, Finbar?' As family, The Greek was inviting Finbar to declare first.

'What are you having yourself, Vera?'

Vera held up the bottle.

'Champagne?' said Finbar, laughing derisively, forgetting himself for a moment. 'Hydrogen!'

'A pint is out of the question,' said The Greek to him, frowning, and a little sharply.

'I know that,' said Finbar, just as sharply. 'I'm not a fool.'

'Any kind of whiskey,' said The Greek to Vera, declaring for himself.

Finbar nodded that he would have the same.

'With anything?'

'Half and half,' said The Greek.

And Finbar nodded, too, to this, and added, 'If you please.'

'I'll get a jug,' said Vera and went out.

The Greek wondered how his father would handle a situation like this one.

'She has the Guards in the town upset, all right,' said Finbar, quietly. The grandeur of the room had an unsettling effect on him, especially that of the bed and its shadows. It could not be a healthy thing to sleep under so dusty-looking a canopy. The panelling reminded him of coffins.

The Greek was examining the décor in closer detail. The panelling on the lower half of the walls was certainly oak but it had been painted over, and then someone had tried to comb the grain of another timber – ash? – on the panels. Why should someone want to turn an oak into an ash, or vice versa? Over the dado-rail there were more panels, spaced in the green walls. These panels had murals painted inside moulded plaster frames: a country church, a round tower – various – all of them with trees of a species known only to the botanically ignorant head and insensitive hand of the amateur who had painted them, and who was dead, The Greek hoped.

'They get very dedicated when they're upset,' said Finbar, referring again to the authorities. He was watching the expression on The Greek's face. It was not right to be inspecting another person's property like this.

The Greek propped his hat behind his cane on the mantelpiece. Over the mantelpiece was something that was meant to be another rural idyll, done by the same hand that had painted the others. This one featured a thatched cottage built on the side of a lake, on what had to be – but the picture was not showing it – marshland, of the kind that has always encouraged a suicidal strain in the Irish peasantry; this one was more detailed than the others and it had figures. The Greek peered closer, hoping that what the leprechaun-like man of the house was doing at the gable end might be relieving himself.

'What?' said Finbar, whispering, wanting The Greek to sit down and talk to him.

'These are most inappropriate,' said The Greek. And moving across the room, doing a full turn without stopping, to look at the ceiling: 'Out of what was once elegance they have made a pig's mickey,' he said without a trace of humour, going into the bathroom.

Finbar felt very small in the chair. If he was in the Imperial Hotel ten times in his entire life it was as much: now he was getting drink in a grand bedroom upstairs. He noted the poor sound-proofing of the bathroom, The Greek's seeming carelessness of it, and he wondered if there was another one on the landing outside.

'There you are!' He shifted in his chair, leaning forward as if to rise, to then sit back in it more tensely. 'You weren't long!'

Vera had returned with a jug of water.

In this setting, he found it hard to believe that he had had her seven times. She looked – what was the word? – luscious. She looked lovely. He had a sensation of pins and needles all over him, but especially in the soles of the feet.

'How's your head?' she said without looking at him.

'Oh!' She was pouring the drinks in that concentrated way of hers: it was difficult to tell if the faint smile was a well-bred way of forgiving him for hitting her or if it meant the opposite. 'Oh, it's!' he said, feeling it. The welt on his head was still sore to the touch. 'That's the first time that that ever happened me.' He wanted to add that he was sorry, to vocalize it, but he had missed his chance.

'Bejesus-begorrah, well ye're a nice pair the three of ye!' said The Greek, coming out of the bathroom suddenly.

They laughed.

And in the next moment he was in motion again, walking fast the perimeter of the room that was available to him, throwing his hands at the murals and marvellously side-stepping furniture because he was looking back at Vera all the time. 'Are you fond of these?' Then, having come to rest and taken up his glass, 'Good health!' he said, soberly.

'Down the hatch!' said Finbar. 'Oh, Jesus!'

They laughed again. Finbar had slopped drink over himself. 'My good coat!' he said. 'Oh, Jesus, I've done it again!' His laughter got out of control. His face was pained.

He became self-conscious of exceeding himself, of being the last one to stop laughing, of being the one who was unable to laugh at all, and then – back to self-consciousness – trying to get himself out of the hole. This was his pattern until he became disgusted at the end of the evening. And he competed with The Greek.

'Isn't this Georgian?' he said. He rolled his head to tell them that he was talking about the entire hotel. 'Is it?'

Vera did not know what it was.

'Queen Anne,' said The Greek. 'But you'd hardly credit it now.

Before that, it was a farmhouse in a field – a grange, don'tcha know. Seventeen-o-seven, I think it was, it was acquired by the Lockes for to build a dower-house for one Maria Locke, my great – to the power of "n" – grand-aunt.'

'Aa no!' said Finbar, crossing himself, a habit of his to pretend he was impressed. 'You're not serious!'

'Mm!'

The Greek elaborated on the history of the dower-house, how bits got stuck on to it until it became a town.

'The women Lockes, especially, who lived here, were hardy – stout, Protestant gels. Every one of them, down to Lou, my benefactress, but not including my mother, could tumble down the finest staircase without loss of a drop to their glasses.'

He paced a lot. He laughed when he shouldn't and became grave at his jokes.

'They arrived and left in the rain, fled silently – and forty thousand others like them in our own lifetime – and no one said stay.'

'No one said go – '

'No one said anything,' he said to Finbar. And then he laughed again. 'But they're all gone now an' there's nothin' more the sea can do to them, the creatures. Though, come 'ere, an' mind you, wait'll I tell ye this: wasn't there a rare sightin' of a couple of them a month ago, huntin' buffalo ablow in the glen!'

Vera was fascinated by him. Everyone else appeared to be so sure of themselves. It was impossible to tell when he was serious or not. The Greek himself, she believed, did not know. It was exciting.

She sipped champagne and the two men worked their way down the bottle of whiskey.

A pause grew longer. It was not because of Finbar's self-consciousness. Vera knew what it was about and she took a sip from her glass as she returned silently to her place, to sit propping herself on the side of the bed.

'Roll up an aul' stone to the hearth,' said The Greek in a quieter

141

brogue than before, in a kind of sigh. He had got up and put his back to the fire. He was rocking himself on his heels and each time he rose he screwed up his eyes as if to draw their attention to the celling or the wall behind him.

'Are you fond of it, Vera? What?' he said, still rocking and screwing up his eyes.

She smiled at the floor.

'What?'

'Oh, I don't know now,' said Finbar, giving his favourable opinion of the painting on the chimney-breast, thinking that was what The Greek was referring to.

'Well,' said The Greek, coming to a stop, 'shall we let the drink decide it or do you wish to declare now which of us you're going to have?'

Vera smiled her slow amusement again. Then she looked at him. His raised eyebrows and the pitch of his head were asking her the question still. With deliberation she turned her head to look at Finbar. Finbar, still in his overcoat, was in a state of suspension, his eyes cast down at nothing.

'It's my birthday!' she said.

It surprised her that what frightened her yesterday did not cost her a thought today. She felt happy. Maybe the feeling would not last. Where she was going from here she had not the faintest idea at the moment. The reasoning process for what she would do with herself and her inheritance would come – if it should come at all – later. Why ruin the moment by thinking about it now?

It was her thirty-eighth birthday and she was enjoying it and there were twenty hours more left of it, and Sunday too if she liked. There were moments during the night when she too walked the room – found herself doing it – waving her arms and rotating her shoulders. She was celebrating her sexuality, nourishing it. But it was not only a matter of her sexuality. If the two men from her hometown, who were sharing her party, both of whom she liked, thought it was solely a matter of sex, then good luck to them if that was what pleased them. That was their business. She felt different. She felt loose. She was not wearing any make-up. In the day that had passed she had shed some illusions, slipped out of folds of the past and, at home, she was tasting the lightness and freedom of becoming herself.

She had moved out to a new place. A lot of things were gone. She might have to find something to replace them. She was on her own. These were moments of pause in her elation. But she was exhilarated. In a way, she felt naked.

She was laughing again: at what, she was not sure; but she could hear the ring of truth in the sound of her voice. In this moment she loved Finbar and she trusted The Greek. Don't ask her why. Sometimes her mind was ahead of her and told her things without her knowing their meaning. Sometimes she got it wrong. She would catch up on her mind later.

It was gone four in the morning. Finbar's speech to Vera was slow. He had a foolish grin, brought on by drink, and he looked mournful. Unlike Finbar, The Greek, outwardly, appeared to grow more sober-looking. At the moment he was pretending to be asleep.

'I'll give you another one,' Finbar was saying.

The Greek's leg shot out from under him. 'I beg your pardon,' he said to Finbar and attended. He was aware that Vera was enjoying him.

'No!' said Finbar. 'Vera! You're given a hundred pounds by your wife to go to the fair and you have to come home with a hundred animals. Now, the animals cost five pence each for a sheep, a pound for a cow and a fiver for a horse. Now, you have to buy some of each and they must add up to a hundred, and – and! – you can't bring home change out of the hundred pounds.'

The Greek blinked. 'What is he talking about?'

'How many of each kind do you come home with?' Finbar's eyes gazed longingly at Vera.

Vera shook her head.

'The only clue I'll give you, Vera, is that you work for a start in multiples of twenty.'

'Stop it, Finbar!' The Greek said sternly. 'This is oral sex, Irish-style, you are engaging in.'

Vera had picked up the two bottles and she was laughing hilariously going out the door.

'Vera!' Finbar called after her. Then, looking lost, 'Where is she gone to?' he whispered to The Greek.

'What about your hounds?' said The Greek.

It took a moment for Finbar to think. Then he became suddenly angry. 'Didn't you see me yourself giving my key and a pound to young Flaherty the footballer to go up and let them out and give them a bit to eat earlier on in The Shamrock?'

'He's not reliable,' said The Greek coolly. 'A seventeen-year-old athlete that drinks as much as young Flaherty the footballer cannot be!'

'I'm not a married man!'

Finbar spoke in anger again and with exasperation. He was worn out all evening, concealing his bitterness about the evening: the way The Greek was trying to move in, playing up to Vera, and – he felt, but he could not be sure about it – the way that she was leading him on. Incest. It was disgusting. Vera was his ride.

'I'm sorry?' said The Greek, his ear cocked. 'You're not a married man?'

Finbar brushed the question away, sullenly, though, indeed, he had a lot more to say. But there you have it: it was all right for The Greek and his likes to speak to you but it was a different matter for you to speak to them.

'What are you talking about?'

'Nothing!' said Finbar. 'You tell *me* what I'm talking about!'

Oh, he had a lot more to say all right. Fucking incest. The country was rotten with it. Brothers and sisters were at it, fathers and their daughters, Christian Brothers buggering the children and then beating them, priests driving round in their Volkswagens screwing

144

young ones and doing their housekeepers. And there was rape. And there were young ones and auld ones getting pregnant and praying to fucking statues about it. There was no love. The country was rotten with sex because that was the only thing it was taught to think about.

Finbar wished he was a bigger man.

The Greek was sitting back in his chair considering something. He opened his mouth to speak but clapped it shut again, and looked away. The difficulty of confiding a matter in Finbar.

Finbar, hands in pockets, watched him.

The Greek looked down and considered again. Then he said, 'A family matter,' and he tapped his jacket. He opened the jacket to reveal the top of a brown envelope projecting out of his breast pocket: 'I have to discuss a matter with her.'

Finbar's eyes dilated. 'You're drunk!'

'I'm?'

'It's half-past four in the morning!'

'I'm!' The Greek was very proud of his drinking prowess.

'I have to go again,' said Finbar and went out.

He had used the downstairs gents twice during the night. He did not need to go again but he was hoping to find Vera down there or meet her on the stairs and put the hard word to her. He had been drinking with The Greek since half-one on the previous day, he was unsteady on his feet but he reckoned he would be all right lying down if he kept his eyes open. He was melting with lust. Just one night more with her was all he was asking for – one-one-one – then she could go and do any fucking thing she liked. Unlike Florrie Delaney, who was brought up on tripe and onions, Vera was brought up on the best.

Equity maxims were spinning in The Greek's head. He who comes to equity must come with clean hands: his hands were clean, his behaviour was ethically flawless in looking for the natural justice of the situation that he found himself in. Where there are equal equities the first in time prevails: the first in time weighed in

Finbar's favour on the scales. But he, unlike Finbar, was carrying his drink: equity regards the balance. And! If he now had the edge on Finbar, that was Finbar's own fault, nobody was forcing Finbar to drink anything: equity will not assist a volunteer. Therefore, when Vera returned with another bottle of whiskey, which was what he expected her to do, two more glasses would finish off Finbar, and, with clean hands, The Greek would ply her with his earnest suit.

He produced a hip-flask and drank from it as he went swiftly to the door to listen for sounds from outside. Truth to tell, the memory of his father, who, after all, was dead for twenty-four years, was wearying. Through Vera, by Vera, in Vera, who was a real pro, unlike a scrubber you might find in Newcastle, he would exceed the deeds of his father and, thereby, hopefully, his own spirit would be able to rest in peace at last in the bosom of his family.

His sister-in-law had immortalized herself in the town today and having an affair with her, over the heart of the same town, would bring lasting glory on him too. It was such a good idea that he was, possibly, already in love with her. Her deportment was remarkable. He had watched her openly and through veiled eyes all night and if she had a single flaw, other than that her shoulders were a little square, a fraction high – as if she were wearing shoulder-pads, which was not the case – he could not see it. Other than that, what could he add but that he was starved of a relationship?

Vera was making up a bed for him in one of the rooms. She had already done the same in the room next door and put out towels for Finbar. Intuitively, she recognized something in The Greek that was kindred to herself. She had of course met him a hundred times before but, tonight, it was like meeting an old friend for the first time. She was very happy about it. The party, though – she judged – was going into a wobble. Two men, one woman. It would be a pity to spoil it. She would tell them in the phrase of her mother's, 'Haven't ye all day tomorrow?' and get them to bed. Or, rather, 'Haven't we all day tomorrow?' because she was going to propose that the three of them should go on an outing, perhaps stay overnight somewhere. They would have a lovely time.

In any case, she wanted only her own company for the rest of the night. It was a strange twenty-four hours that had passed. She had a feeling that she was about to catch up on her mind and she was ready to hear how far it had got.

'Come in.'

It was ten past six. She had heard him padding across the hall from his bedroom to the bathroom a couple of times in the silence of the previous hour. Now he had knocked on her door. She extinguished her cigarette.

'Come in.'

He had removed the hard collar and he was in his shirt-sleeves. Galluses supported the dark striped trousers that she noticed earlier were, like the jacket, turning green. He was in his bare feet and one hand was concealing something beind his back.

'I forgot,' he said, producing a letter from behind him. 'I was asked to give you this.' He was very unsure and appeared to be waiting for an instruction. 'It's from your brother, Tom, and your sister, Mary Jane.' Then, as if her impassive face had enquired about the absence of Marcia's name, he said, 'Marcia?' He could not tell her that, in this business, Marcia was no more than a pilferer. He shrugged a shoulder, dismissing Marcia as a force. 'They're using her,' he said.

She inclined her head towards the bedside table and he approached and put the letter on it.

'I should not bother to read it. I steamed it. It's a horrible composition.'

She let her eyes rest on the letter, kept them there. Her kindred spirit gave off waves of loneliness. His smile was painfully vulnerable.

'I married the wrong sister.'

She nodded sober agreement to this. Then she looked at him and asked: 'Can I talk to you about something?'

The Greek was preparing to sit down.

'No. I mean, on Monday morning,' she said.

'Sure.' He was puzzled by her.

She looked at him again. 'If we go on this outing tomorrow, might they have us locked out when we get back?' She saw his lips part. She continued to look at him candidly: did he not know that there was a practical side to her nature?

'It's a possibility.'

She picked up the letter and continued to look at it.

'Well, goodnight again.'

He left, head bowed, returning to his room.

One thing she had always known about The Greek was that he had married the wrong sister. And Mary Jane should not have married Declan Mansfield.

He had not opened the letter and neither was she going to open it. She let it slip through her fingers on to the floor because, whatever its contents, it would not change by one whit what was going on in her mind.

One. The weekend to be enjoyed. Two. Finbar for sex. She was feeling broody. What more fitting conclusion to the defiant story of Romeo and Juliet, that had begun twenty-four years ago, than that Juliet should have a baby? Without Romeo ever knowing a thing about it, of course. Three. The Greek was known to be a kind of St Jude of the legal profession. He defended hopeless cases. He would advise her.

(ii)

'Did Henry stay the night?'

'I believe he did.'

'Is he up?'

'I don't know,' said Vera, 'I'm just going to check.'

It was eleven o'clock and she had come in to wake up Finbar.

'Would you like a cup of tea?'

'I can't drink black tea.' He was peeved at the idea of it.

'I've been out for milk.'

'I don't mind so.' Then, as she was going out the door: 'D'you want to bring it up or will I come down?'

'Get up!' she called from the hall. 'And have a bath!'

As far as she could tell – because she had not bothered herself to look at them – the Saturday morning people on the Square were unnoticing of her when she crossed it an hour ago. Today, the morning sky was dull and grey. She bought the local newspaper, milk, brown bread and a packet of disposable razors in Lynch's and, in Clancy's next door, two locks similar to the ones on the hotel door. It was no big job to her to change locks. The two shop assistants in Clancy's were moving to stand together as she left the hardware shop. That was all.

Breakfast took its mood from the sky despite Vera's efforts. But she was never much good conversationally. The celebration and hilarity of the previous night was a questionable memory; it might not have happened. A morning after nothing.

The Greek wore a perpetual frown and his eyes washed the table in an absent way, as if in search of a memory or a prop. His jaws shone in the perfect shave of an alcoholic. Vera was not putting a bottle on the table. She had been house-bound since last Monday and if drinking had to be done it would have to be done outside of the hotel.

'It's Saturday, isn't it?' said The Greek.

'All day,' said Finbar. He had had several cups of tea and was pouring another one, and, now that he had consumed his toast, he started into The Greek's which had gone untouched. 'There's dog-racing tonight in Newcastle.'

'That's a good idea,' said Vera, 'but let's go somewhere now.'

Life, if not enthusiasm, came into the brief discussion that followed in the form of simulated interest for lunch in Newcastle, a look at the sea, a night at the dogs and whatever else chanced their way.

'We shall trust to circumstance,' said The Greek. And this reflected perfectly Vera's attitude. It kept the matter open and adventurous.

The mode of transport was decided on. Vera's car was not mentioned. For one thing, it belonged to a parcel of problems that she was having nothing to do with until Monday morning and, for another – tacitly understood by the three of them – it was parked too close to the reality of The Greek's home.

'Synchronize your watches,' said Finbar. 'I'll be back to pick you up at twelve hundred hours.'

He knew that it would be closer to thirteen hundred hours but he did not want The Greek to think that he had all that time to be alone with Vera. He left to borrow John-John McNulty's van and, on his own behalf, to engage a temporary kennel-master for Cleo and Tina.

The pace of the binge was what was wrong. Thus, The Greek rationalized his present state of futility. The rhythm was not as he would have it, had he been in charge. What he had been thinking about Vera last night was stuff and nonsense. Well, it was close to stuff and nonsense. Something of it lingered. Faint music in the soul. But what was he meant to do about it, what was he meant to do with her now, this minute? She looked very attractive last night. Perhaps she was equally attractive now: how was he to know or judge on that? Her body – her parts – moved a great deal more this morning in her fawn woollen twin-set, in a maternal kind of way. Perhaps his interest in her was Oedipal. Whatever it was, it was inconvenient. And it was probably unfair to Vera. And was it worth it? Was anything?

Vera went upstairs to find a suitable coat to wear. The atmosphere was far from relaxed down there. The Greek had avoided meeting her eyes but she knew he was watching her. Already, he was a friend of hers: she had decided on that. But there was something the matter with him and she did not want his confusion. Finbar's complexes were enough to be getting on with. Look-look-look – lookit, if you like – they were going out to have a lovely time. For God's sake! She was determined that her weekend plans were going to work. Yippee? Yippee! 'Tck!'

Finbar was late. They left the kitchen too soon and sat for a while, waiting in the cheerless expanse of the dining-room. In the kitchen she could, at least, pretend to be doing something. They waited in the lobby and she tried to read the local newspaper but put it down again when she came across a notice about the auction of the hotel. The Greek picked up the paper. The coat she had chosen did not suit the twin-set and she went upstairs again and exchanged the twin-set for the blue dress.

When Finbar still had not come, she idly flicked through letters that had accumulated in reception. Among them was one for herself.

'In connection with the estate of your late grandmother, Winifred Sarah Lally, we should be obliged if you would call to our offices at your earliest convenience.'

There was something strange about it. The address? Buffers' Lane, Newcastle. It was dated two months ago and was signed by a Pádraig O Siadhail, who called himself a dlíodóir, which, obviously, must mean solicitor. Mom had a few hundred pounds in a post-office book and had left it, or part of it, to Vera: perhaps that was what it was about. She would deal with this too, next week. Heigh-ho!

The doorbell rang and was followed by a dramatic whisper through the letter-box from Finbar. 'Finbar!' Vera was becoming annoyed.

In the confined space of the vestibule, The Greek took her hand clumsily and kissed her. She held on to him for a moment because he was trembling, and it disturbed her.

The get-away van was backed almost on to the pavement and Finbar was opening the back doors as they came out. The Greek got into the back which was not what Finbar wanted. He did not want Vera plonked beside him in the front, driving through the town, but that was where she was sitting. The Greek knelt on the mattress in the back of the van, his arms on the backs of the seats, propping him.

They got away slowly. Traffic was heavy. It being a Saturday, the country people were in town. They walked in the middle of the street, they thought they owned the place, they would hardly get out of your way. 'They learn it from the cattle,' said Finbar.

Going down the busy High Street, they saw Marcia's large figure coming in the opposite direction. She was bothered and was puffing in the exertions of manoeuvring her pram on and off the pavement through the crowd. She did not see them. Vera watched her as she might have watched a stranger. She was protecting herself. The Greek turned his back and sat on the mattress. He had not thought to find himself blushing, and feeling sorry, guilty and resentful, all at the same time. He took out his hip-flask though he knew it was empty.

Before meeting the Newcastle Road, Vera glanced up at Tom's house on Cnoc Mhuire. When Tom was at home his car could be seen parked outside the house. He was not at home.

'We stop at The Half-Way House, lads?'

'Yes,' said Vera and The Greek in unison.

The countryside opened before them.

'And who is this fine big woman?' The three of them laughed. Vera and Finbar had a pint of Guinness each in The Half-Way House, The Greek had a pint of lager and he got Mrs Folan to fill his flask with Bushmills before leaving. 'And which of ye owns her?' said Mrs Folan.

The rattling of the van was music in Vera's ears. Rhododendrons, intermingled with fuchsia and gorse, were breaking in the hedgerows. In long gaps on either side, miles of bogland climbed towards the hills. Vera let down the window. The Greek passed his flask forward. She was smiling, she shook her head, her eyes were closed, smelling the turf and the heather. 'I don't mind if I do!' said Finbar.

Posters pinned on trees announced music in singing pubs and signboards on legs advertised hotels. They were approaching Newcastle. 'Oh, look!' said Vera. 'A circus!'

They were unaware of Tom watching them. He was about to get into his car to set off for home when he saw the van pulling into the car park. He ducked. (His father-in-law and mother-in-law had a grand, big house in Newcastle and he visited them on a regular basis. On this occasion, however, he had called to say that he would be collecting his children, whom his in-laws were minding, on Wednesday. Tom would require them for the auction on Thursday.) He watched them getting out of the van. If he was not mistaken, his sister was wearing one of his mother's dresses. It was certainly his mother's coat. He watched them moving across the car park and going in the back way to Griffin's Hotel. His sister appeared to be trick-acting, laughing and flaunting herself, and he never felt such shame for her as he did now, since she appeared to have none for herself. But now he had to get back home to Grange where he had a meeting with Tommy Martin, his solicitor, and with Mary Jane, who was behaving like a flaming viper, at a quarter past three.

The Greek ordered a plain omelette. They had asked for the menu to be brought to them in the bar. Finbar said he did not want anything but Vera said, 'My treat,' and ordered a steak for him and Irish stew for herself.

Heads turned when they came into the dining-room. The curiosity was The Greek, his period suit, cane and the black hat that he had only a moment ago, for whatever reason, put on for a first time today. He was talkative again and he spoke at length and learnedly about acupuncture and the fluid in the spinal column. People at other tables looked at one another.

Finbar ate voraciously, his face inches from the plate. Vera's deportment, which had so impressed The Greek the night before, was most odd. She did not appear to realize that she was copying everything that Finbar did, his worst manners. And when The Greek had a single slice of white bread, no butter, with his omelette, and Finbar said something about the importance of soakage to the drinking man, she seemed to find it – and everything else that Finbar said – extraordinarily witty.

Children surrounded them en route to the Fair Green. Some of them thought The Greek was part of the circus and, outside the Big Top, the bravest, a little girl, ran up and touched him.

Vera was thrilled by the circus. She sat between Finbar and The Greek. When The Greek offered his flask, she smiled no thanks, and when he pushed it further to offer it to Finbar, she whispered, 'He's okay,' without ever taking her eyes off the ring. Occasionally she clapped her hands together, silently, in delight.

The Greek was struck by the childlike wonder.

'Aren't you sorry for them?'

Vera shook her head, smiling, watching the lions. Then, as if hearing what he said only now, her face slowly became grave and she looked at him and then back at the lions. They looked cared for, well-fed; they were not bored. She looked at Finbar and, though his smile of fascination continued fixed on the animals, he said, 'It's not right, all right.'

The Greek was sorry that he had spoken because her concern continued.

But then came the next act. A baby llama and a baby camel stood in the centre, blinking show-biz eyelashes as their parents – two camels and two llamas – went through their paces. Vera pointed and nodded at the babies to draw Finbar's and The Greek's attention to them. 'Animals won't breed if they're unhappy.' Now her head was inclined towards Finbar, as before, and she was happy again.

The Greek was very glad to be in their company.

Best of all and top of the bill was a clown's act. The clowns' timing was mind-boggling. It was wonderful. Everyone left happy.

154

'Yeh see, yeh see, these two clowns come in,' they said – Finbar, Vera and The Greek – in pubs and in the streets as they made their way across town, explaining to people why they were falling about and laughing.

'Yeh see, yeh see, these two clowns come in – with this big square box – to deliver it to a third clown – and the box has to be opened, yeh see – to see what's in it – and they open it – oh, Jesus, Mary and Joseph – a Jack-in-the-Box jumps up – his arms shoot out – boxing the ears of the others – but yeh see, yeh see – they retaliate – and he gets out of control – Jesus, Mary and Joseph – and there follows – and there follows – Jesus – a series of hittings – missings – duckings – swipings and misunderstandings!'

'Yeh see, yeh see, these two clowns come in.'

The dogs was a financial disaster.

'We back the favourites, I suppose?' said The Greek.

'Not tonight,' said Finbar, the expert.

He was drunk on himself and he was drunk on the attentions that Henry Locke-Browne and Vera O'Toole were paying him as much as on alcohol. In his pride, he would not even look at them when they spoke or when he spoke to them. They had to do the looking. He was aware, also, of a few car-loads of people from home attending the meeting, who were watching his sophistication; he was glad of this because he did not give a shite for anyone in the whole country. He might have been hearing messages from the race-card the way he had it curled, with the point of it in his ear, while he looked into the middle distance. He said things like, 'Madame X has early foot and if she hits the lid to make the bend in four-point-five, which she's capable of, all the others'll be looking at is her arse,' or, 'See here, Stansvasia was bred in the purple, out of Mersey Dote and Brylcreem, he's well-drawn in number 6 because he's a wide runner, so you may forget Julius Caesar.'

'Sounds Welsh to me,' The Greek kept saying and Vera laughed admiringly while they backed Finbar's selections, and lost.

Vera did not care.

They made their way back to Griffin's Hotel and she managed to book two rooms for the night. She took Finbar's arm and whispered that they should not stay too long drinking in the lounge, that the two of them might slip off upstairs.

He did not like women throwing themselves at him. He slipped his arm out of hers, sat on the banquette, produced handfuls of coins and other objects and put them on the table. It was all right for Miss O'Toole and Mr Henry Locke-Browne but he was skint. He had three fivers in his back pocket that he was saying nothing about.

The bar closed down and the lounge thinned out until there were only themselves left and a party of red-faced men, two of whom were priests, and a chain-smoking woman in an anorak, whispering in a corner. Finbar took a dislike to them and made comments about them in undertones. Vera recognized them as a party she had seen at the dog-track. Finbar had taken a dislike too to the young night-porter who fetched drinks on a tray. In his white shirt, black trousers and green dickie, he looked like something that should be step-dancing at a fucking feis. And Vera was crowding him again, and the Greek, her brother-in-law, was lamping it all, and weren't there plenty of seats for her to sit on besides being nearly up on top of him?

'My charmer,' she whispered in his ear.

My fucking charmer! It was a disgusting thing to see a woman behave like this in public.

The Greek had remarked to himself on Vera's demeanour over lunch. Now, it was as if, unaware of herself, she was performing some kind of mating ritual. Every few seconds her head touched Finbar's shoulder, she hugged his arm to her side and rotated her body against it, she hunched down into herself, in the next moment she stretched outwards and upwards, to then crouch again, to put her breasts on the table as if offering them to Finbar on a salver. It was most odd. He would, he felt, have played a decent Herod Antipas to her Salome; Finbar looked like a sour John the Baptist whose halo had slipped down behind his raincoat.

The party of red-faced men and the pale chain-smoking woman went out, and the young porter started to clear up.

Vera's hand was under the table.

The Greek held his last tenner in his hand. He had tried to cash a cheque earlier but the young porter said that everything was locked up and the best and only thing he could do was serve drinks for cash. 'Young man!'

The young porter was pretending that he had not heard the summons.

'He should be whipped!' said Finbar. 'Whipped' came as a sudden yelp, like a small cry of pain. 'Sonny!' He jumped up, rattling the glasses on the table. He was in a rage but he did not know if he was permitted to shout and, now, he was hissing across the room at the young man's back.

'Speak when you're spoken to! Obey!' And he was not consistent. 'We're not blacks, yeh little bollix yeh! And we're not Connemara people either! We're fucking residents!'

He looked at The Greek and sat down. 'Fucking residents, aren't we?' he asked reasonably, hoping for The Greek's support and approval of this assertion of their rights.

The Greek held up a hand and was about to speak, but, 'Oh, I see,' said Finbar, getting up again, 'I see! The Lord is my Shepherd!' He did not know what this meant but what he was trying to say was that he believed himself to be completely friendless.

The young porter continued to calmly clear the tables. He was only four months doing this job but he had already formed the opinion that at least half the men in the country were as dicked-up as that old bollocks who was now going out to the gents. Whatever had done it to them, he had no idea.

En route to the gents, Finbar noticed a chair that was lying on its back and he stopped to set it upright. 'By Jesus,' he told the chair, 'it wasn't by the Christian Brothers, anyway, or priests either, that he was trained or learned his manners!'

The Greek had a word with the young porter and got him to fill his flask while Finbar was in the gents. The keys of the van were on the table and he took them. Before leaving, he said to Vera: 'There is nothing so futile as planning for pleasure. Goodnight again.'

(iii)

Walking along here yesterday, Vera said she loved the breeze but that the idea of the sea frightened her, and Finbar agreed. It's big, all right.

The Greek was walking the prom again. His mother told him that all babies cry at their first view of the sea but that when she had taken him, as a baby, to this very place in Newcastle, he had laughed at it. Though the sea still had no fears for him, he had come down in the world since babyhood.

He was thinking too of Marcia and his children. Why was he walking a deserted prom on a Sunday morning, twenty-eight miles from home? He knew that he was special, but being special meant more than being an oddity or an anachronism and he could not think what it was. Where was the place for him to be? The sun was trying to come out from behind the clouds and he bared his teeth up at it in a kind of grin, in the way that his father used to do it. Fathers are quite unnecessary. What did his wife and children mean to him, or he to them?

His hand kept returning to his chin. What he dearly wanted was a shave. He felt dirty after the night spent in the van, but he would settle for a shave for now. There was still an hour to kill, however, before any place opened up, before he could go back to Griffin's Hotel.

A friend of his from student days had packed up suddenly one day and run off to join the merchant navy as an ordinary rating. Scrubbing decks was how The Greek pictured him, though they probably had machines for that kind of work, even back in those days. The Greek had had a card from some far-off place from the erstwhile philosophy student, his friend, the sailor. The message on the card was an over-simplification of how to cope with life, but it was an appealing one. 'A sailor's problem is to get from A to B. The boat takes him.'

The surface of the road through the quays area was uneven and he walked the outer lip of it, which was granite, the edge of the wharf, past rusty tugs and barges. The boats appeared to be stuck rather than sitting in the water. He turned his back on them and on the hungry wheeling seagulls and he counted five church towers of one kind or another, rising above the town. He set off again, up a narrow street of derelict warehouses. There was another church up here somewhere.

He had not taken Communion since the morning of his wedding, thirteen years ago. He had taken it with a clean conscience. The night before his wedding, he had a party in Elm Park, mixed – he did not believe in those rugby-playing stag affairs – and there were lots of glitterati there, with the exception of Marcia who was superstitious about being seen by the groom on wedding's eve. At one point he slipped away quietly and was gone for the most part of two hours. Where he had been for those two hours was his secret still. On a sudden emotion, he had hired a taxi to Newcastle and got it to wait on Main Street while he went off to have a chat with a friendly Benedictine who blessed and absolved him. He did this, not because he believed in the church but because a lot of his guests and all of Marcia's guests and friends did, and, in receiving Holy Communion with them in the morning, he would feel clean of conscience, knowing that he was not offending against them and their folk customs. Or so he told himself. Extraordinary. He thought he would try it again this morning.

'The Lord be with you,' said the Celebrant. 'And also with you,' the assembly responded. God bless the work, and you too. Stop.

The church was full. A lot of people got out of their beds, put themselves out: when had the Sabbath ceased to be a day of rest? The Celebrant paused in the ceremony to blow snot into

159

a handkerchief. Stop-stop-stop. 'Michael row the boat ashore,' sang the choir and thought itself charming the ears of the angels. Stop, he told himself, stop. The choir is fine, it's adequate, and this was once, probably, a fisherman's church, so the song is perhaps appropriate.

'The night before He suffered, He took bread – ' the Celebrant was saying. The Greek ran ahead in Latin, ' – accepit panem in sanctas ac venerabiles manus suas, et elevatis oculis in coelum ad te Deum Patrem suum omnipotentem.'

They threw out the dark sound of the Latin, sent Michael in his boat out to sea with it to dump it. 'For this is my body,' and 'Hoc est enim corpus meum' sank with only a few bubbles to show for itself. Stop. But he could not stop. 'Hic est enim calix sanguinis mei.' Was there something deeply wrong with him – Art thou troubled? – that everywhere he looked he saw ugliness? He was sick of himself, heartily sick to death of himself. He knew that if they said – potato – he would say patato. 'Lift up your hearts!' Brassières. Let's call the whole thing off.

But, instead, he joined the long bread queue. He found that he was frightened. This was serious. They might refuse him. It would be hard to blame them if they did. He warned his face to find the correct expression, it was looking too eager and betraying him for what he was.

Communion used to be a great time for watching nubiles and mature women in clean jewellery in parade, to and from the communion rails.

His turn was coming up. The man on his right took a sip from the cup and the Celebrant wiped the cup where the man's lips had touched it. The Greek watched the Celebrant's eyes and he knew that he was not going to be refused. He took a sip and the cup moved on to the lady in the headscarf on his left. They had done away with the wafer – there was a touch of Greek Orthodox here – and he selected a corner of bread from the basket that was held in front of him by an acolyte. A much nicer idea than the wafer, he thought, and he returned to his place with the bread. But he could not bring himself to eat it and he held it in his fist. Then, not knowing what else to do with it, he put it in his pocket.

The people continued to file to and from the altar for bread and wine.

Four years ago, London, he was given a ticket for a cup final at Wembley Stadium. Chelsea and Leeds. He was not interested in football. The predatory sounds of sixty thousand fans roaring before the game. Then the band in the middle struck up 'Abide With Me' and, in seconds, sixty thousand predators became victims, hushed in a rendering of the hymn. It was so beautiful. It moved him beyond telling. A brother and a sister, Carlos was their name, in a nightclub in Madrid, danced a flamenco. He was not interested in dancing but he waited to watch them dance again in a second performance later in the night, and he went back on the following night and, each time, the ritual of the young brother and sister in dance moved him beyond telling. Yesterday, laughing out loud at the clowns – laughing – had the same effect on him, and on Vera and Finbar too, he thought.

'My dear brethren in Christ.'

The Greek sat up. 'Do not let your hearts be troubled.' 'You know the way to the place where I am going.' The gospel of the day that he had listened to, earlier in the Mass, had interested him. The homily, he hoped, would expand on it. 'I am the Way, the Truth and the Light,' the gospel had said. 'If you know me, you know my Father, so how can you say, "Let us see the Father"?'

'My dear brethren in Christ,' said the homilist, 'though Christ is not physically present, as he was during his life here on earth, he will perform "even greater works", as the gospel tells us, in the Church. And the message we should draw from today's gospel is the role that we all have to play in the Church. Christ was the precious cornerstone of the Holy Catholic Church, we are the living stones of that edifice. We are, all of us – today as never before – a royal priesthood, a consecrated nation, a people set apart to sing God's

161

praises and to do His blessed work on earth. How do we live up to it? Let us go back to Christ's own words in the gospel. "I am the Way, the Truth and the Light," he said. Christ was no fool. "I am the Way, the Truth and the Light." Christ was not a man to speak without thinking. He chose his words carefully and wisely, three words. The Way, the Truth, the Light. He spoke those three words clearly. Let us choose three other words. Contraception, divorce, abortion.'

'For the birds,' said The Greek, glancing at his watch. 'I must arise and go now.'

And he arose and went out of the house. And because he still had time to kill before returning to the city, he went down to the waters again to gaze on them. 'Are ye troubled, are ye weary?' Thus he spake aloud to the birds for many things were weighing heavily on his mind. And the birds to a gull cried, 'Yea,' three times, for all they had partaken of that week was a J-cloth soaked in grease and three small plankton. And a great silence came upon them as they did watch him with their eyes. And then the man brake bread from his pocket and scattered the crumbs upon the waters. And all of the birds to a gull swooped down to see what it was was in it. And seeing that no miracle had been performed and how little it was was in it, 'Bejesus, 'tis worse things are improving, like!' saith the chief gull whose name was Seth. Then all of the birds to a gull did break wind and they flew away to the lands of Uk and Us and to the seventeen corners of the earth where they were sullen. And then the sun appeared to give the man from Attica a sign. And the sun knew the man and the man knew the sun. And the man departed the waters that were oil and salt for he had learned that his end would come in waters that were fresh.

(iv)

If possible, Vera wanted to be present at the moment of conception

in mind as well as in body, to be body and soul united in the
pleasure of an act of creation, and not be just merely coping with
the mechanics of flesh and bones on top of her, with someone
relieving himself of his bag. Having a man poking her was work.
It was a good idea to have a baby and she was more committed to
it than ever. She would pursue it earnestly. She had applied herself
too eagerly last night. Too eagerly, at least, for the type of person
that was Finbar. He was embarrassed for her, among other things.
Last night took a long time but she continued to operate on him
– which was not the way she wanted to have to do it – until,
eventually, she got him to come inside her.

They were sitting in the lobby of Griffin's Hotel, she and Finbar,
waiting. She turned the pages of her newspaper in order to glance
at him. He was still cross with her.

'Parties Deadlocked Over Contraception', 'Government Hesi-
tates', 'We Shall Meet The Government On The Issue On Wednesday, Please God – Bishop'. It was all above Vera's intellect.

Strange to think, she had had only one serious, adult relationship
ever (and that was with Wally the Swede). That intimate bond
and her childhood romance with Finbar were the only significant
friendships in her life. And that appeared to be her lot. A lot of
men wanted to have a relationship with her but she always shook
her head. This was strange too because she had always craved
affection. Maybe, like Finbar, she was incapable of receiving
affection, or of dealing with it. Finbar now, as a man, was
incapable of having a relationship with anyone. He was a bachelor,
confirmed, selfish; and she was the same, destined and wanting to
live alone. Heigh-ho!

'Backbenchers Will Oppose Any Proposals To Allow Contracep-
tives To Be Sold Openly To Unmarried People.' Sometimes, when
she got a brief on a client, she read a newspaper or a magazine
to see if she could learn something by heart and use it to get over
her difficulty with conversation. Now she wondered might she ask
Finbar for his opinion on which was best, selling condoms over or

under the counter, just to break the ice that was between them. She decided to remain silent. It was not a subject he would want to discuss with a woman at the best of times, let alone in the morning and when sober.

He was cross with her because she did not wake him up for breakfast. She had let him sleep on because he was looking wrecked.

'Why didn't you wake me up?' he said. He got very annoyed. Breakfast was over. 'That's how they make their money!' he said. 'I can give you book, chapter and verse on the Griffin family! You paid out good money for bed *and* breakfast!'

She glanced at him again. She was very fond of him. And she was amused. She knocked hell out of him last night. She was amused at herself and she felt like laughing. Tonight they would have beautiful sex. She would play it differently tonight.

The tin-roll of the shutters being pushed up in the bar could be heard as The Greek came in the revolving door to the lobby.

'By Jesus – ' said Finbar. 'What? – but you're well able to time it!'

The Greek broke into laughter at the sight of Finbar and pointed at him; his body threatened to fall over. Finbar laughed too. He was so glad to see The Greek. Such a greeting! They hugged each other.

'Afternoon, Vera!'

The Greek cashed a cheque at reception and they went into the bar. He was not a wealthy man. It required careful management of what his aunt had left him as well as Marcia's resourcefulness for the family to get by.

'What are you having, Vera?'

'Virgin Mary.'

'Finbar?' He laughed again at Finbar's aspect and hugged Finbar's shoulders. 'The reins of your bowels are instructing you to be merciful! What are you having?'

'I'll have a vodka, Henry, make it a double.'

The Greek laughed in celebration of the folly and he ordered the drinks. He was having nothing for himself as yet, he had first to see to his toilette. He produced a razor and went out to the gents.

They collected the van. There was a pub on the other side of town that Finbar had heard about but had never stood in, and they went there. Vera drank mineral water. It was an unsatisfactory session for the men – four drinks – and they were outside again, standing by the van, at half past two. Sunday licensing laws were uncivilized. The pubs would not be reopening until five o'clock. They were keen to get down to some serious drinking: where would they go for the next two and a half hours?

'Home?'

The Greek shook his head to her suggestion and Finbar looked at her: who was asking her opinion? He – Finbar – resented, also, that she had drunk nothing alcoholic.

In her opinion, Finbar was not looking well and she was being protective of him.

'Drive us back to Main Street,' said The Greek. He had an idea: Boxer Tierney's.

They could hear people getting drink inside in Boxer's and though they knocked and rang the bell and tapped various codes on the glass with a coin, they were not being allowed in. They drove out to Rancho Mick's. Mick himself, in studded belt and cowboy boots, answered the door. 'Ye can fuck off back to wherever ye were drinking all morning,' he said. The day was suffering from lack of pre-planning. Publicans do not like customers who only arrive for the holy hours and drink the licensed ones in other people's houses.

'Something to eat?' said Vera.

'I thought we came out for a bit of sport?' Finbar challenged her.

They drove around the streets of Newcastle longing for the inside of a pub. They drove in circles, returning to the same streets, time and again. The Greek had his flask but this was no good to Finbar

THE SEDUCTION OF MORALITY

as he did not want the taste of whiskey down on top of vodka. In one street there was a crouched, mongrel sheepdog who, every time they came by, jumped out at them, chased the van and bit at the tyres. Finbar was out to get him and he kept going back to the street, accelerating and braking to intensify the dog's anger, keep his attention on the wheels of the van so that he would forget the parked cars up ahead and run himself into them.

'Could I have a drink, Henry?' said Vera.

In the half-light of the back of the van, The Greek was trying to make out an article in the newspaper about the cherished values and the quality of Irish life that were under threat. He closed the newspaper and sat on it. 'Grotesque, bizarre,' he said, reaching the flask to her. 'Unbelievable!'

Finbar was unsuccessful with the dog but he nearly struck disaster to the van. The shock of what had nearly happened to John-John McNulty's property wiped his mind clean and out of terror came inspiration.

'I have it!' he said. 'I know where we can go! Mrs Folan is a good old skin. I'm sure we'll get a drink in The Half-Way House.'

Mrs Folan was good to them. They arrived at The Half-Way House at five past four and they left it at ten past twelve that night. She gave them bacon and cabbage too. Vera ate heartily. The Greek only touched his and apologized to an understanding Mrs Folan. Finbar ate greedily though he knew he was making a mistake. Mrs Folan, he believed, did not wash cabbage – but he needed the iron – and she cleaned the knives on the dog's back.

The Greek had never driven a car. They assisted Finbar into the back of the van and Vera drove it home. During the journey, Finbar moaned a few times. Vera concentrated on the road. There were patches of fog and at times she felt that she was moving slowly in the clouds with nothing to hold on to but a wheel. The Greek, in the passenger seat that had been hers, appeared to grow taller with each successive mile and he was bolt upright by the time they pulled up on the Square in Grange. He felt completely sober, and he continued motionless, staring ahead at the reality: nothing. Vera thumped the steering wheel with her two hands, banged her forehead on it and laughed into herself in some kind of release. The engine waited, idled.

'Would you like to come in?'

'Home!' A moan from the back of the van. And a plead: 'Please!'

Vera threw her head back and laughed in a light-headed way. Then she drove to the New Estate.

Finbar was like a blind man, his hands searched about him in paddling movements and, alternately, they kept brushing Vera's hands away when she came to his assistance. He looked jaundiced. Like a rag that had been boiled to get the stains out, she thought. And she laughed again. The Greek got out of the van for no other reason than that the engine was switched off and he stood by. Finbar was going in his gate; his hands, behind him, were still brushing away assistance, brushing away mankind.

'What about the van?' She was holding up the keys.

Finbar did not want to know. He had enough to think about in steering himself to his door, and he was shaking his head without looking back at her.

'Well!' said Vera when Finbar closed his door, and she got into the van.

The Greek followed in an automatic way, and they drove off.

'May I come in?'

'Sure. A nightcap.'

In the kitchen she indicated that she would have a small one with him. He raised his glass. Then, on reflection, he shrugged: he had nothing to say. She nodded, and became grave for a moment. He sipped, shrugged again, this time to himself: there was not anything worth talking about.

'Well!' She knocked her drink back, one go, and got up. She indicated the ceiling to tell him that his room was upstairs if and when he wanted it. 'Goodnight!'

She could hear him standing up as she went out the door. She did not have to look back to know that he was bowing to the table: 'Goodnight again!'

He disturbed her and when she came down a half-hour later to see how he was, he was still standing at the table with his back to the door. The bottle was held aloft in his two hands and he was making signs with it and whispering.

'Hic est enim calix sanguinis mei novi et aeterni testamenti.'

He became aware of her presence, returned the bottle to the table, and sat down. He opened his hands, held them apart, then left them on the table to show that he was docile.

The line of least resistance was not always a bad thing; sometimes it was the wise thing to do, and she came and stood behind him. She put her hand on his shoulder and, when he began to cry, she caressed his face and wiped his tears. 'Come on.'

XII

THE DRUDGE

All week, in the terraced crescent of Elm Park, the view of the silver Merc from the living-room window of The Greek's house was a heart-scald to Marcia. She often closed her eyes in the hope that when she opened them again the car would have vanished, and she was harsh with the children because she hated Vera. On Wednesday she stopped her eldest three from going to school; Norman, Winnie and Belinda. She had only seen her husband once since Friday.

He came in on Monday, three o'clock in the day, and straight-away went up to change his clothes. 'Hell-o!' was all he said, and that was to Joan and Mary Frances, and that was because they were playing in the hall and he had to step over them. Not a word to Baby Carol or herself. Then, when she heard him going up to his study on the top floor, she went up to the bedroom with Baby Carol in her arms to smell his clothes. Baby Carol was as good as gold, Joan and Mary Frances were playing in whispers, and now

169

she regretted the severity of her warnings of what would happen to them if they were not good: she wanted them to start crying for her. Of course she could not be sure and it went round and round in her head, 'It's nothing personal, it's nothing personal,' but what else could it be? Vera wanted everything.

In the near-silence of the house she could hear him on the phone to someone and she went down again to see who it was. He was arranging a meeting with Tommy Martin; he was acting for Vera. Then he rang the National Bank to arrange about a loan: not for himself, for Vera. Then he called Dublin, the Hertz crowd, about the scuttering car. It was during the next call, to Martin A. Costello, that Baby Carol blew a gurgle into the mouthpiece when Marcia lifted her hand from it to wipe the tears from her nose.

And sure she would not have said a word to him had he given her a chance. In fact she had a nice cold lunch hidden in the fridge.

'You're going out again?' she said when he passed the living-room door without coming in, and by the time she found the courage to go after him and call, 'When will you be back?' he was half-way up the street. He hardly shrugged his back. The leather patches on his sleeves she'd sewn on for him herself with her own two hands, going out of the crescent. It was shocking.

Six times on Monday night she put on her coat and took it off again, thinking to go up and brazen it out with them. There were things that Henry liked in bed and it grieved Marcia sore to think of anyone but herself giving them to him. And he told her more than once she looked best without her clothes on. Then she phoned the Imperial. The heart within her breast was like the tip of a rusting nail. Vera answered the call on a laugh as if to mock Marcia's wretchedness: Marcia replaced the phone slowly, her mouth opening ever wider in a silent scream.

Then, and it must have been one o'clock in the morning, the phone rang. 'What-what-what is going on?' Mary Jane, without preamble, in her abrupt manner. It was too much to bear and Marcia burst out crying.

170

'How yeh doin'!' Tom called in person, Tuesday morning. She told him she didn't know where she was, but all he wanted was to quiz her about Henry. Then he phoned Mary Jane and they had a three-way discussion, with Mary Jane in the middle, represented by the phone. They were only out for themselves, as far as Marcia could see; they were no more interested in her than the cat. Commitments and family values were only so much talk. It was all about the hotel, the auction, The Wool Stores. 'I only want Henry to come home,' was all she wanted to tell them. Then a row broke out. Mary Jane was eating the head off Tom. 'Why-why-why amn't I kept informed about developments? Why-why-why?' Tom had just said that Henry had threatened to have Tommy Martin investigated and that Tommy Martin was now suggesting that they – he and Mary Jane – get another completely new solicitor entirely.

For a brief moment Marcia hoped. She prayed. If the whole matter were to be about Tommy Martin's professional, moral and social fabric, and not the things that were going on in her head, then life would return to normal and all would be well again when Henry had him struck off the Roll of Solicitors. Marcia would never forget the evening they had Tommy Martin in for drinks because he had just come to live beside them in the crescent, three doors down. His father shot the crows for the Locke-Brownes: that kind of work. Nevertheless, Henry had him in, to welcome him. Before he left that evening he offered to buy their house and furniture. Marcia knew that Henry had never forgotten it.

But, when Henry didn't come home on Tuesday night either?

On Wednesday – what else could she do? – she told the eldest three they could get up all right but that they were not going to school. And they stayed upstairs for the day. Baby Carol was crying on the floor in the kitchen. Marcia had put on the kettle to make a bottle. Then, while waiting for it to boil, she wandered the length of the double-room, from the kitchen to the living-room window, to stare out vacantly at the crescent. Vacantly, it seemed, and with dulled senses, because when she held up her fists, felt them shaking about her ears, she thought it was to shut out the noise of Baby Carol. Then she realized what it was, that it was Vera, coming into the crescent, wearing her mother's clothes and swinging her bag. The clothes fitted her. They had been promised to Marcia, but what good were they to her, except for cutting up? Vera wanted everything. And Marcia turned her back to the window. She looked about the room, the floor, walls, the ceiling, the length of the room and into the next one, wondering what was it she was looking for, until she found it. Then she went out with the steaming kettle.

She nearly had Vera. Vera was beside her car, one knee lifted, with her bag on it, searching for her keys. She froze at the sight of Marcia. Then she ran for it, trying to contain her bag that was hanging open. Marcia pursued her, the length of the crescent, to the Newcastle Road, on to it. Vera, trying to cross the road, was nearly knocked over. It was lunchtime; traffic was heavy. But now the cars were stopping as Marcia followed Vera along the centre of the road. Then Vera escaped into the High Street and Marcia stood there, the kettle at her side, her chin dipped, crying.

In the crescent of Elm Park a sudden rage overcame her again at the sight of the silver Merc and she ran at it, raising the kettle to bring the heel of it down on the car. She saw the lid come off. A scalding pain streamed up her arm. Then it stopped for a moment. Then it started to return, slowly, and, as it did, she raised the kettle again and poured what remained in it over her other arm. Life was unfair, it owed her more, she deserved better.

Winnie, Belinda and Norman watched from an upstairs window. She saw them and she waved them back. She could hear Baby Carol crying from the kitchen. She wondered what Joan and Mary Frances might be up to. She bent down for the lid and felt her head become big in a rush of blood. She continued stooped over, hoping that her head would burst and end the drudgery, servility, degradation, the shame and embarrassment of her life.

Inside, she tried running cold water from the tap over her arms but it made the pain grow more intense. Her arms were heavy, fleshy, and had become ulcerated from the boiling water. She could not think what else to do and she sat down, looking at Baby Carol. Baby Carol screamed back her own frustration.

Then Norman, Belinda and Winnie came and stood in a little group in the doorway. First Belinda, then Norman, came into the room. Winnie continued in the doorway, standing in formal support of them. Belinda had started to hum one of her own tunes, she picked up Baby Carol and started to dance with her in circles, and danced with her slowly out of the room. Then Norman said to his mother, 'I'll phone Dr Kelly, please.' She shook her head. 'Please.' This time she heard him, she thought about it, and she nodded her permission. 'Call your Uncle Tom first,' she said, 'and your Auntie Mary Jane.'

She knew how to fix Vera for good.

XIII

THE AUCTION

The hotel had been the venue of many a sale in its time: now it was preparing to auction itself. It was hard to put your finger on it but Finbar thought there was a bit of danger in the air for someone. He would not be here at all today only for what he was doing now: The Greek had asked him to prepare the dining-room and he was arranging the furniture like you might for a concert, and he had already created a makeshift dais at the head of the room for Mike Hammer to stand on and be seen by everyone.

The last few days were frantic, with Finbar driving The Greek around the countryside and into towns, sometimes as far as sixty miles away, sticking up posters, leaving fliers in places, and such-like. And drinking during it and in between. Jesus, Mary and Joseph, The Greek was some man for it!

The Greek himself had plastered all the windows of the hotel with posters announcing the auction. No fear of the occasion being as loud as this had Tom O'Toole and his solicitor, Tommy Martin, had their way. And Tommy Martin, they were saying now, was out of it.

The Greek's determination in the whole matter puzzled Finbar. Finbar knew of course that The Greek, now, too, was knocking off Vera, every chance he got, but it was not for that alone that was making him so – ardent. Maybe what was in The Greek's head was running off with Vera when the money came through after the auction. But then, again, it was hardly that: there was a look about him that did not bear the elopement theory out; and, also, The Greek was soft about money. Of course, at one time, the hotel belonged to the Lockes, the mother's side of the family, and maybe it was that. But only maybe: The Greek would not strike you as being that bitter and revengeful. Unless, of course, he was better able to conceal it than Finbar's intelligence realized. What? No. He wasn't that cute. But there was a look about him that was charged with fire: at the same time there was something lost in the look. He was like a man driven to fight for very good reasons but who could not remember what the very good reasons were. But Finbar reckoned The Greek would drop any day now. Jesus, Mary and Joseph, the man would have to lie down!

Anyway, it would be starting shortly.

The Greek, Hammer and Martin A. Costello were having a final meeting in the lobby. It was twenty to two by the clock. Bodies moved across the windows outside and, occasionally, a face, with hands blinkering itself, tried to peer in. The door was shut and it was not to be opened to anyone, on The Greek's instructions, until five to.

'Should there be a low call,' The Greek was telling Hammer, 'it should be treated with the scorn it deserves. Martin A.?'

Martin A. nodded his solemn old head.

'The dignity of the hotel and its vendor cannot be insulted,' said The Greek.

'Please God,' said Mike Hammer.

175

These were difficult people that Hammer was dealing with. They were talking principle. It was rumoured that, between them, they had enough on Tommy Martin to crucify the man six times over for malpractice, so, Hammer had to watch his step. Old Martin A. was nothing if he wasn't an honest solicitor; he was legendary for it. Hammer was not entirely certain about The Greek, though.

But he had no sympathy for Tommy Martin, or for Tom O'Toole either. He had several dealings with them, the pair of them. The Sacré Coeur, for instance: he handed that place to them on a plate and, instead of receiving a reward, he had to fight tooth and nail for his bare two and a half per cent. He knocked down a farm of land to Tom O'Toole, most favourably, very nice, and, when it came to his commission, he was knocked down himself to one and three-quarters, and he had to wait fourteen months for it.

So, Tuesday afternoon, when The Greek arrived in the sweetshop and said, 'If you want to handle this auction you will forget any instructions you have had from Tommy Martin or any other party because I am now in charge: do you have any problems with that?' he could answer at once, 'None,' because he was delighted. And he stood to make decent money for a change.

'None,' he said immediately to The Greek. 'How,' he said, 'can Tommy Martin act for Miss O'Toole, the vendor, and for Mr O'Toole, the purchaser? How? The positions are ridiculous because they are contradictory.' A mistake.

'*Do* we,' said The Greek, 'know who the purchaser is going to be? *Do* we?'

'No.'

But then he mentioned the names of a couple of other possible purchasers, and he redeemed himself completely, he felt, by raising a matter that The Greek had overlooked.

'Yeh know,' he said to The Greek, 'the Aga cooker is not technically a fixture. Did you know that? Not in this case since there's another means of cooking in the kitchen. What?' The Greek did not know it. 'I don't suppose,' said Hammer, 'you have much idea what one of them would cost a man today? Do you? Even a second-hand one?' The Greek nodded to him to continue, to make his point. 'Yeh know, Henry, the contents of that place are worth an awful lot of money, an awful lot, and should we, really, lump them in with the sale of the building, the way Mr Martin and Mr O'Toole wanted it to happen? What?'

The Dutch people, he told The Greek, had the right idea. In Holland, if a man or woman sold their place, they did not leave a lavatory seat behind them. Fact.

'I'm talking twenty-five thousand pounds-worth of stuff. What? More,' he said. 'Maybe as much as thirty with the help of God.'

The Greek gave a right slap to his forehead on Tuesday because the contents had not entered his head until then. People would make you laugh.

'Well, that's about it,' said The Greek. He looked at the clock, and got up. 'Let's have a look at the room. I'm very confident.'

Maybe The Greek had arranged a puffer: Hammer hoped to God that he had. If he could have talked straight to them he would have a couple of puffers in the room to make a right auction out of it. 'Please God,' he said, collecting his papers.

For a change, the day outside was consistently bright and sunny and it was very warm. Even so, some of the women were over-dressed and, for afternoon, the older ones were wearing too much make-up. Knots of people had gathered, and the O'Toole family – three cars because of the children – were parked in the South Mall.

The interest of course was almost entirely curiosity. The resumed hostilities among the O'Toole family since Vera's return from the United States of America were common knowledge, as were the dramatic events surrounding her occupation of the hotel. It was of course public too that The Greek had become her legal advisor and maybe something else as well, and that he had engaged Martin A. Costello to act on her behalf in conjunction with himself. And, indeed, some of those waiting outside the Imperial now had actually witnessed Marcia's attempt to 'roast' Vera in a public street, yesterday.

When the door opened at five to two and those who wanted to went in, the attendance numbered a good seventy, not including the children. They began to settle themselves. Hammer and Martin A. stood at the very top of the room beside the dais. The Greek kept to the back wall for the moment, beside Finbar. He did not want to look Marcia in the face; he could not. All she would want, he knew, was a smile; it grieved him that he would not be able to manage it.

He watched her back go up the room with the children and the others. Tom, Caitriona, Mary Jane and Declan. He watched them become seated around the top two tables, all their chairs facing the dais. They continued isolated there.

Caitriona looked around at one moment and caught The Greek's eye. She was nervous but she looked bright; she was off the pills; she smiled at him. She was carrying Baby Carol for Marcia. The Greek did not reply; he was frowning at the upright, well-behaved backs of the seated children. They might have been in church. Norman, Belinda, Joan, Winnie, Mary Frances, Martina, Joe, Aisling.

The gathering favoured the bottom half of the room, increasingly from about centre-way to the back wall. The doorway was choked, and there were others in the passageway, content there to listen to the proceedings and wait for the outcome in the half-dark.

Martin A. began to read pieces from the deeds and, when it was necessary, he explained them. The Greek left Finbar and tiptoed halfway up the room to a chair which he positioned so that he could observe everything that was going on, front and back, his shoulder angled to the window-wall.

Finbar continued buried in the end corner, the one across from the door. It suited him to be concealed. There was a bit of tension in the air, all right.

'Is she here?'

Mrs Kelly was on tiptoes in front of Finbar, balancing herself with her fingers on her husband's shoulder. 'Is she here?' she was whispering in his ear. Her question might have been referring to Vera or Marcia.

Dr Kelly, Mrs Kelly's husband, was a very quiet man and he continued eyes front, not replying to his wife's question. He should not be here either – he was not that kind of man – and there was something here too that was puzzling Finbar. Dr Kelly was a dedicated man. Conscientious was another word for him. He took a fatherly interest in his patients. He had children of his own, and a mother and father too, one time. He was born in Argentina. His lips moved constantly, as if he had a pulse in them. Finbar was puzzled.

Yesterday evening they were in the kitchen, Finbar, Vera and The Greek, and the doorbell rang, and Vera asked Finbar to go out. There was Dr Kelly. 'Could I see Vera, Finbar?' he said against the timidity of his mouth. He never spoke much above a whisper. But Finbar reckoned him for a man who would do his duty no matter what. Then, when Vera had seen him, and it hardly took more than a minute, and came back to the kitchen, it was not Finbar's place to ask her what he wanted, but, 'What did he want?' said The Greek. 'He said I'd like you to do a test,' says Vera. 'What kind of test?' 'He didn't say.' 'What did you say?' 'I said I'll do any test you like for you if everyone else in the town does the same test.'

That was the length and breadth of the interview because, apparently, then Dr Kelly only looked at her for a minute, nodded, and he left. The Greek gave a bit of a laugh, all right, at what Vera said to the doctor and got back to whatever matter he was advising her on before the interruption, but Finbar wasn't so sure. You had to remember that Finbar himself was lifted one time and locked up, and by saying, 'I'll do any test you like for you if everyone else in the town does the same test,' maybe Vera had done the test. D'yeh see what I mean? Maybe that was the worst possible thing in the world she could have said.

It was not that Finbar did not think Dr Kelly a good man – the contrary: he was full of admiration – the man was a saint, he was sound as a bell; it was that if, say, a matter were to come to arbitration with Dr Kelly presiding, the individual did not stand a chance against the family.

Information was the doctor's wife's nickname in the town. 'Is she here,' she was whispering again, 'Vera?'

The doctor was the kind of man who hated nosiness but he had to respect her as the mother of his three children who were all doing well. He shook his head.

Vera, all right, had gone out of town for the day on The Greek's recommendation. Proper order too for the vendor of such a property: it was dignified not to be hiding in a closet, upstairs maybe, or hanging about, waiting, with her tongue stuck out a mile. The Greek was going to phone her with the news after the auction.

'Are there any questions?'

Martin A. had completed his end of things and Hammer was asking on his behalf if anyone wanted anything to be further clarified.

'Are there no ashtrays?' said Mrs O'Driscoll, who attended most every function that happened in the town and who was not afraid to speak up. 'Have we become Americans or what?' she said. 'Are we not meant to smoke?'

Hammer looked down the room at The Greek. The Greek as the overall director of operations had been calling the shots, down to the details.

The Greek did not change his expression. 'There are ashtrays,' he said with measured blandness, then he looked over his shoulder out the window and made a yawn of his mouth without actually yawning.

Everyone in the room heard Marcia trying to stifle a sob at this. How passionless the sound of her husband's voice! How unfeeling he had become towards her in the space of less than a week! The swiftness with which life can change was alarming. Every married woman in the room was side by side with her spouse excepting the widows and Marcia. She wished now that she had not burned her arms because in this moment she needed to hold Baby Carol. She began to rock in her seat.

'Still!' said Mary Jane to her in a hiss, pressing her fingers on Marcia's arm.

'Ufffff!' Marcia winced in pain.

'Sorry,' said Mary Jane. 'But-keep-still!'

Geesstupid! Mary Jane was in no mood to be trifled with. She was sick to death of them all. Tom, Marcia and that bitch-in-heat – or whatever was up with her – Vera, were making an unholy show of her as well as themselves. Why-why-why – when it was her nature to do business with people on-the-spot – was she part of this ongoing circus? Why hadn't she, six months ago, a year ago, offered Tom fourteen thousand pounds for The Wool Stores? Fifteen, sixteen thousand pounds! So much time and effort wasted! Now he had her. If, now, she did not play it his way, he would sell to a stranger before he would sell to her – even maybe if she gave him seventeen and a half. Mary Jane was in a car that was being driven by someone else.

Mary Frances and Joe had started trick-acting. 'Take them out – take them out!' Mary Jane hissed at her husband, Declan. 'Take them outside and give them an ice-cream!'

Declan left, obediently, with the two offending children.

'Well, if ye're all supplied with ashtrays,' said Hammer, 'can I continue?'

'What about the contents?'

Very nice. 'Thank you,' said Hammer to the tough-looking woman who had spoken. 'I was just going to mention them in the conditions of sale.'

Tom's heart skipped a beat at the tough-looking woman's question, the first threat to the property he considered to be his, but he did not look back to see who the woman might be. His smile widened a fraction to then freeze again. He was slouched in his chair but his body was rigid. His neck was gone once more. His fists were clenched, one of them concealed in his trouser pocket, the other one like Robert Emmet's. The only things that moved were his eyes: they appeared to be swimming over the mask of his face. When morality goes out the door anything can happen.

People were craning their heads to get a look at the tough-looking woman who had spoken and to wonder who she was. They did not know her. Hammer knew who she was: the mouth on her like the top of a hot-water bottle. Very nice.

He was holding up a sheaf of papers. 'We have here with us,' he said, 'a complete inventory of the entire contents of the hotel.' He stood to make two and a half thousand, approx., out of the contents. Five per cent from the vendor, five per cent from the purchaser. But the contents were unlikely to be sold today. Maybe. 'And after the sale of the hotel, at an appropriate time, we'll first see if we can deal with the successful bidder for them. Thank you.'

He mentioned some other conditions of sale and then concluded: 'Finally, folks, there is no reserve price on this wonderful property. Therefore, it'll be sold today. Therefore, can I ask, when I open the bidding, that nobody here will not extend the same civility, faith and dignity, that the vendor places in ye, by making any stupid offers.' He considered that he handled that one well. 'The highest bidder will make a deposit of twenty-five per cent before leaving this room and will sign this contract. Thank you. The hotel is now on the market and will be sold on the drop of the hammer.'

He tidied his papers and continued to look down at them for a moment as if gathering his thoughts in a silent prayer. He loved this moment in an auction, even in the ones that he knew in advance were only a waste of time. He felt like a priest at the consecration time of the Mass.

And the congregation might have been preparing to kneel. They shifted in their chairs, they cleared their throats and coughed, and those on their feet shuffled them until they found the correct stance: until there was stillness.

'Who'll start me off?' said Hammer.

Stillness. In their expressionless eyes it might have been that mankind, as represented by this small assembly, had heard that hope was gone.

'Who will start the bidding, who will start me off? Ladies and gentlemen, it's twenty-nine minutes and thirty seconds past two o'clock, ye heard Mr Costello etcetera and so forth on the deeds, ye heard myself explain the conditions of sale, so, everything is clean, so, who will start the ball rolling? I'm a very busy man and I have to be somewhere else by three.'

Some of those present were grinning now.

Hammer covered the room, avoiding looking at Tom O'Toole as yet. He felt that this would be the way The Greek would want it for now. He knew that The Greek didn't trust him. Fair enough: and as he told himself earlier, he was not so sure that he trusted The Greek. The Greek was not a stupid man.

Hammer knew his job. Before The Greek had spoken to him on Tuesday, what was meant to have happened was that he, Hammer, would suggest an opening bid of, say, sixty grand, Tom O'Toole would nod, then the brief formality of a look around and the hammer would fall to Tom O'Toole. But, new ballgame. Hammer had an auction on his hands and he knew it; he could smell it.

'Who wants first blood?'

He told them a funny story.

It was still likely that Tom O'Toole would get the place – for a price – but it was no longer a foregone conclusion. He had, now, he knew, two other possible purchasers sitting in the room. Maybe more, because he himself had spread the lie that Tom O'Toole was no longer interested in the place, that, as everyone knew, his wife, Caitriona, 'the doctor's daughter', was unhappy living in Grange; as everyone knew she had decent-sized problems; that the entire family was moving to Newcastle; that if Tom O'Toole was going to throw in a token bid or two it would be out of shame or honour; who can give you reasons, who can tell in cases like this? Wise men never try.

He raised his eyebrows a little as his eyes glanced over the tough-looking woman who asked about the contents. She was a Miss Lamb and she had come from one of the three neighbouring counties. Now! She was a member of a family that already owned three hotels in the province and was said to be behind Dolly's, a restaurant in Newcastle. They were empire-builders in the making in the catering trade. Maybe she was only interested in the contents. Maybe. He thought not. Her face was formidable. Very nice. She was built like a small tank.

But a more welcome presence in the room was Robert Carney's. Rubber Head. He was on Hammer's books. He was looking for a property that would impress people. He had told Hammer that, not alone would he not bid for the place, it was most unlikely that he would attend the auction. Now!

He was six months back from England, where he had made a fortune in an Irish dancehall. He had arrived home with a Cork lassie whom he had set up presently in a flat in Newcastle. He was married and everyone knew he was undergoing the throes of a long wait on an annulment from Rome, that the fancy woman, the Cork lassie, was getting fed up waiting, or she was pretending it, and nothing was too big for him to buy for her. And especially if it was a place in his hometown because, though you would never call him ostentatious – he was a quiet man – it stood to reason that he wanted to show people. The home he came out of, the Lord save us! Poverty? Desperate entirely.

Even before he left school he had started to wear the cap. Alopecia did not leave a rib of hair on him anywhere. And the sister, the binneog. He hated going to Mass because he had to take the cap off in church. But he went, and he prayed. Three or four times a week he visited the slaughter-house yards in the town to drink hot sheep's and cow's blood. The lads knocked the cap off him at the pictures, they thought he was a fool, and they called him Rubber Head. Then he emigrated, the one most likely not to succeed ever in anything. Now, here he was, seated – Hammer was glorying in him – the two hands on the knees, the head down, contemplating a patch of floor, the wealthiest man in the room, possibly maybe in the town. They said it was his discovery in England of the toupee, which could be worn in church, that had done it and, with the exception of the one mistake, marrying an English lassie, he never looked back. Very nice.

''Tisn't every day a property like this comes on the market' – Hammer kept up the patter – 'and 'twill be a long time again before its likes comes up for sale! Ye'll all be rushing in a minute – who wants the honour? This magnificent property, this magnificent, valuable and historic property, a going concern, what am I bid? What am I bid, the lovely day that's in it outside!'

Under normal circumstances, at this stage, Hammer would be picking flies off the wall, imaginary offers from the back of the room, to get things going. Instead, he chanced a fleeting glance at Tom O'Toole. Tom pulled back the leg that was outstretched, as if he was doing it to clear his throat. Hammer saw The Greek become alert. The Greek had been watching Hammer's every move and gesture, now he was watching his brother-in-law like a hawk.

'Well, this is one shy company,' said Hammer.

It was time to look at Tom O'Toole directly, he judged, and he did so. Tom's face reddened, then he started to jack himself up in the chair. Then, in this same moment, The Greek was on his feet, turning to the window-wall to unfasten one of the top panels and, as he did so, a voice from the other side of the room said, 'One hundred thousand pounds.'

Tom's face cracked and then it froze again into a wider smile of fear. Caitriona smiled sympathetically at him. She kept smiling. This weights-and-measures husband of hers was driving her around the bend. How was she to keep putting up with it? Another course of medication, hit the bottle at home again? How unbearably lonely

185

and boring it was, drinking at home! Marcia looked more alarmed than her brother and, except for the white blotches, her face was no less coloured than his. She was sweating. She was wearing an overcoat because it was the only garment in the hall, before she came out, with sleeves wide enough to cover her bandaged arms from the public. She fanned herself with a bit of paper, stopping when she remembered that the movement was annoying Mary Jane. Mary Jane darted back a look at the young man who had put in the opening bid.

'The car is out of control,' she told herself.

They knew this young man, and they knew his father well. The father had slaved for him to supplement the scholarship for university. A small farm, about thirty acres, four or five miles outside the town. The young man was a young solicitor who had qualified last year and who was, for about a year, courting a girl in the town, one of the Heneghans, Assumpta. He had already begun to neglect her for the company of his seniors, people like The Greek, aping their life style and their manners without the right to either. He fancied himself as an urbanite, he too was given to quotations, and a sticky end was waiting this precociousness was the forecast. In surface material he was more in the line of a barrister with the airs he put on. After all his father's trouble, his father did not know what to make of him.

The young man enjoyed the attention that was being given him. He spoke in a clipped, authoritative voice, not at all the accent of the area, and flicked ash from a black cigarette on to the floor. Presently one thumb was hooked in a waistcoat pocket. The only person not to acknowledge the young man was Robert Carney: he was in a position to do so but he did not as much as lift his head, and because of that, and because the young man had been seen on the previous night, taking a drink with Robert in The Shamrock, 'Aha!' said the people in possession of this information, 'he's acting for Rubber Head.' Wrong.

'Aha!' said Hammer to himself, 'The Greek, the hoor, has engaged him as the puffer.' Very nice. Maybe.

'We're off, we're off!' said Hammer. 'I'm bid one hundred thousand pounds, one hundred thousand, I'll accept it – who'll give me one hundred and ten, a hundred and ten? This is a very valuable property – who will give me one hundred and ten? I won't say we've started at the bottom of the ladder 'cause I'm not a greedy man, so I won't say that – who'll give me a hundred and ten? We've started somewhere approaching halfway, and can I suggest that from here on in each rung of the ladder will cost ye ten thousand at least so as not to be wasting the lovely day that's in it in here – one hundred and ten! – the unsettled weather we've been having. I'm bid one hundred thousand pounds, who will give me one hundred and ten – anybody?'

Tom realized now that what had always been his strength had become his weakness: his tendency to trust too easily in others. 'And one,' he said.

'And?'

'One.'

'I'll accept it. I'm bid one hundred and one thousand pounds – here in the centre – I'll accept it – who'll advance me on that?' Hammer was enjoying his powerful position. 'Who'll give me a decent advance on that? Now's yere chance to get in the race – if ye're not in ye can't win!'

'One hundred and eleven,' said the young man.

'I'm bid one hundred and eleven thousand pounds – here on my left – one hundred and eleven thousand,' said Hammer, hoping, please God, that if his surmising about the young man being The Greek's puffer was correct, the young man was not going to get carried away with himself and overdo it. 'I'm bid one hundred and eleven thousand pounds – this is more like it because this is a wonderful opportunity for someone. Any advance? Tourism is booming – the place hardly needs a lick of paint or if the successful bidder has grander ideas there's government grants going abegging from Bórd Fáilte.'

'And one,' said Tom.

'I'm bid –' said Hammer.

'Twenty,' said the young man.

'I don't follow,' said Hammer.

'Twenty,' said the young man. 'I'm raising you eight on one hundred and twelve.' The cigarette was now held between his teeth, giving him a confident grin. He had his jacket swept behind him and the flats of his hands were on his kidneys, in the manner of German officers in the pictures.

'I see,' said Hammer. 'I'm bid one hundred and twenty thousand pounds on my left.'

'And one.'

'One in the centre, I'm bid one hundred and twenty-one thousand pounds.'

'Eight.'

'I'm bid one hundred and twenty-nine thousand pounds – my left.'

'One.'

'I'm bid one hundred and thirty thousand pounds.'

'Nine.'

'I'm bid one hundred and thirty-nine thousand pounds.'

'One.'

'I'm bid one hundred and forty thousand pounds – the centre. Does anyone else want to get in the race?'

'Six,' said the young man.

'One hundred and forty-six thousand pounds – my left.'

'One.'

'One forty-seven thousand pounds.'

'Four.'

'One five one thousand pounds.'

'One.'

'One fifty-two.'

'Six.'

'One fifty-eight.'

'One.'

'One five nine.'

'Nine.'

'One sixty-eight.'

'One.'

'One hundred and sixty-nine thousand pounds – the centre.'

'One.'

'One? One seventy thousand pounds – my left.'

'One.'

'One hundred and seventy-one thousand pounds.'

'Eight.'

'I'm bid one hundred and seventy-nine thousand pounds.'

And The Greek, who was standing since the time he opened the window, the time that the young man opened the bidding, sat down at this point.

'And one,' said Tom.

'One eighty thousand – the centre.'

The young man dropped his cigarette-end on the floor and he commenced to roll the sole of his boot over it, carefully.

'I'm bid one hundred and eighty thousand pounds – the centre,' said Hammer.

The hot room waited. Those at the back were up on their toes.

One hundred and eighty thousand pounds was good money for a place like the hotel in Hammer's estimation. It was the figure he had put on it on Tuesday when asked by The Greek. He no longer had any doubt that the young man was a puffer; The Greek's sitting down a moment ago was the signal to stop pushing up the price, to get out.

'I'm bid one hundred and eighty thousand pounds, do I hear any advance?' He was trying to keep his eyes off the young man.

The young man now had the backs of his hands, fingers entwined, on the top of his head, his eyes contemplating the ceiling. 'Ahm!' he said with something of the manner of The Greek.

The Greek's frown deepened.

'And four,' said the young man.

And The Greek, as did Hammer, knew that the young man had lost the run of himself.

'I'm bid one hundred and eighty-four thousand pounds – my left,' said Hammer.

'And one.' Tom had to be the last bidder or he might lose the place. (He had no intention of paying for it.)

'I'm bid one hundred and eighty-five thousand pounds,' said Hammer.

The young man put another black cigarette between his teeth. He struck a match – 'Five' – and lit up.

'And five – and five – I'm bid – I'm bid one ninety thousand pounds.'

'And one.'

'One ninety-one thousand pounds.'

'Five.'

'One ninety-six thousand pounds.'

'And one.'

'One ninety-seven thousand pounds.'

'Two.'

'I'm bid one hundred and ninety-nine thousand pounds.'

'And one.'

'I'm bid two hundred thousand pounds.'

The young man flicked ash from his cigarette, then he looked down to see where it had fallen.

'I'm bid two hundred thousand pounds,' said Hammer again.

The young man picked his trousers, both legs, to dust the toecaps of his shiny brown boots. Then he looked up, thrust the cigarette back in his mouth and shook his head.

Hammer called to the room for an advance on two hundred

thousand pounds and got none. 'Sold!' At the drop of the hammer the place was knocked down to Tom O'Toole – the centre.

Tom never felt so ashamed of his hometown as he did in this moment. He could cry his eyes out but he would wait until he got home; then he could cry his fill.

The under-bidder, the young man, was the first to come to him to offer his congratulations. Tom reared up and all but hit the young man; Tom even surprised himself. His face was like that of a man about to burst a blood vessel. He turned away, but only to find Hammer stepping off the dais with the contract and a pen.

'What's all this?' said Tom. 'What's the rush for?' Though he was talking to himself, he was talking out loud because the other part of his mind was trying to think. 'Hold your flaming horses there!' They were trying to catch him out. Sign a contract for two hundred thousand pounds, is it, and a cheque, now, for twenty-five per cent of that?

'Man, Tomeen!' This was Father Billy's smiling face and broad shoulders, come with their congratulations. Father Billy had arrived late, was caught in the doorway and did not want to interrupt the proceedings by tiptoeing up the room to sit at the top with the O'Toole family, which was what he had promised to do.

'Are you flaming mad, Father?'

'I don't know what you mean, like?' said Father Billy, taken aback. Indeed, momentarily, he was hurt.

'There's much work to be done in Ireland today,' said Tom, reprimanding Father Billy, 'to protect the Catholic ethos!' And he walked away. He hardly knew what he was saying at the moment. Still, in his way, he was vocalizing the concern of the majority.

Father Billy was uncommonly good-humoured and in the next moment he was clapping his hands, laughing with a group of elderly women.

There was a lot of movement happening.

Hammer, urged on by The Greek, had pursued Tom and was cornering him again. Tom rounded on Hammer. 'Martin A. made no mention of the Bank having a right-of-way through our porch,' he said, 'there was never any building permission granted for the new extension, and – and! – the auction sure was twelve minutes late starting!'

This was both heated and in confidence to Hammer. Tom was not thinking properly yet, but he was getting there. The auction was over, he was the top bidder, but he was signing nothing. There was another way to go about it.

It was then that Marcia fainted. The heat, the overcoat, the wretched thing her life had become.

Tom hit a slap to the papers in Hammer's hand. 'D'yeh not see me sister on the floor!' he said.

Declan had returned and he lent his support to Dr Kelly in getting Marcia out to the porchway, thence to the yard. Tom led the way importantly, carrying a chair. Mary Jane followed with another chair, the children and Caitriona.

Mary Jane did not need Declan's pocket calculator to work out that as per her agreement with Tom – the 13:1 ratio and the clause obliging her to pay his stamp duty – The Wool Stores could now cost her twenty-seven and a half thousand pounds, plus six per cent of that for her own stamp duty if the deal was done up front. For a shed! Inwardly, she was fuming. The O'Tooles! And how long had she been telling herself that anything that did not add to her life should be subtracted from it?

Of the children, Norman remained. He stood close to his father's leg. Mr Hammer was facing his father, papers held out in his hand.

'That's okay,' his father was saying. 'I'm very confident.'

Norman wished he could understand why the family was fighting.

'Everything is going according to plan,' his father was saying.

Norman did not think that everything was going according to plan because his father did not appear to realize how tightly he was holding Norman's head against his hip. Then his father told

192

Mr Hammer to wait there for Uncle Tom while he went off to make a phone call.

Finbar had started to rearrange the furniture to how it had been originally. Jesus, Mary and Joseph, it was like warm cream! No wonder they were fighting.

And Norman went out to the yard where his mother was seated on a chair. Dr Kelly was sitting on another chair, facing her, watching her colour returning. Uncle Tom, Auntie Mary Jane, Uncle Declan, Auntie Caitriona, his sisters and cousins were all waiting silently.

XIV

THE LAND OF HEART'S DESIRE

Vera was driving from Newcastle to Glenora village. It should have been as simple as that. No. Slow tears caught in her eyelashes; they would not flow; she had to squeeze them out to restore her vision of the road, thick lenses of them. She drew in deep, silent breaths and kept forgetting to exhale until she felt her breastbone about to snap in two. Of its own accord her head moved, side to side, until, shaken out of it by a pot-hole, it began to nod: then she would think that if she had someone to drive the car for her she could hang the thing, her head, in the back window.

Everything was up in the air again. Worse. She had a sense of foreboding. Worse. She was driving the road from Newcastle to Glenora village and, less than half an hour ago, she had just had the best piece of news in her life. Until half an hour ago she did not know she had a heart's desire. Not alone did she have one, it had been granted to her! Instead of being ecstatic she was heart-broken.

The kettle yesterday? Child's play.

Her mind, again, was awash in a complex of thoughts and emotions, none of them of sufficient clarity or vigour to make an issue of itself; all of them threatening to paralyse her. If something was holding the lot together it was a sense of fear. She prayed her childhood prayer to her guardian angel because who else could she turn to until she saw Mom.

'O angel of God, my guardian dear, to whom God's love commits me here, ever this day be at my side, to light and guard, to rule and guide. Amen.'

The confusion began to purify itself, to reduce itself to a chill about her heart.

The same feeling had touched her at moments during the week. A cold unseen. She kept shaking it off. She had awoken to it on Monday morning. The hotel was never before so silent. It seemed there was not even a ghost left in the place, and that was bad because, if that was so, something else had entered. The usual noises came from the Square. The only sound in the frightened air was The Greek's breathing beside her. Was that what it was, The Greek? For God's sake! And she got up because there was work to be done, business. She was not going to be cowed by a mood, not at this stage. The Greek was a man, like any other. She had taken him to bed because she thought he was suicidal, that was all. And she drew back the drapes and let the light in.

She let the light in and opened the windows because she was looking forward to this week as never to a week before. Her life was changing remarkably. There was an impatience within her to get on with finalizing what she had begun. She was on the threshold of moving out into an extraordinary adventure, going out into a clean elsewhere that, she felt now, had always been waiting for her. She was going to make the break from here complete, leave no loose ends that could become tied again and draw her back. This meant bringing perspective to bear on her situation: this

195

meant dealing with her unwanted inheritance, getting rid of it in an objective, fair, equitable way.

She woke up The Greek.

'Vera?'

Yes, that was who she was; told him to put his clothes on.

His expression asked had they done it and, taking advantage of this lapse of memory, she shook her head.

'So, no damage has been done,' he said.

Against her better judgement, she picked up one of his garments that were scattered on the floor, reached it to his outstretched hand, he caught her wrist and pulled her into the bed. Oh, for God's sake! Why make excuses for doing it? And, as far as she knew, the whole human race was suicidal. Then he did a dance in front of the window.

He seemed surprised when she told him she wanted to sell the hotel; he seemed to think she was enjoying being the proprietress. She did not tell him that the past, as represented by the hotel, was gone forever. She did not tell him everything. And she had only wanted to ask for his advice, but:

'So, the auction is to go ahead,' he said. 'I like it. I'll take the case. Those who thought we would not dispute the matter will now know better.'

She noted his use of the plural, the 'we'. She was making a stand, not to do battle, to do business. But she nodded. She listened to everything he said and mainly what she did was nod.

'The best way to look after the needs of others is to look after your own needs first', 'I should not speak to any of them until the auction is satisfactorily concluded'.

He organized everything. The only matter she did not hand over to him was the letter from the solicitor in Newcastle – the dlíodóir, Pádraig Ó Síadhail – about what, she supposed, was going to be a small bequest from Mom. It was a little strange, and it was personal to Vera.

'Round figures?' said The Greek to her. 'Two hundred thousand pounds for the building and its contents.'

She nodded.

'I thought it would bring a smile to your face?'

It didn't, because she was thinking what to do with the money.

'I'd like my brother to have the place,' she said. And then she added, 'If possible.'

She worked out what to do with the money. When the hotel was sold, the money would be split four ways: a quarter each, for herself, Tom, Marcia, Mary Jane. If Tom bought the hotel, his quarter would be knocked off what he paid for it. And, if possible, she thought that it would be nice if they all had a drink on Sunday night, to say goodbye. Civilization.

And she took The Greek's advice and got out of town for the day. Today.

She was on her way to Glenora village to see Mom. Well, to 'see' Mom. And she was frightened.

Being chased by the kettle? Yes, that was quite a shock. But that was open warfare, you could deal with it. You ran, as you would in New York. It was child's play compared to fighting a cold unseen. How do you deal with that?

And Vera had gone to Newcastle for the day. Done her shopping, bought some clothes, a cake, booked her flight for Monday morning, had lunch, established where Buffers' Lane was, the address of the solicitor, Pádraig Ó Síadhail, and, then, waited in the appointed place, Griffin's Hotel, at the arranged time for The Greek's call with the news.

The hotel was sold, it wasn't sold, Tom had bought it, he hadn't bought it, he hadn't signed, he would sign, someone would sign, someone would buy it. The finality of the clean departure that she had planned! Her last state was worse than the first.

Worse. The nightmare was only starting. She was listening to a man telling her that she had inherited *another* property.

She was sitting in the little office in Buffers' Lane, off the Old Corn Market, in Newcastle, four o'clock, and the little man with the natty moustache, with the bun of curls, in the Donegal tweeds, was telling her that she had inherited her grandmother's farm. Impossible, she told him. He reddened: he was angry with her. He had the will in his hand. It should have been the time to weep for joy at being alive in a world that was making sense in the end of all. She sat there stunned. By no means was it impossible, he told her, and waited to pounce on whatever she said next.

'But my brother has inherited it!'

'Has not! – He has not! – Inherited it.' He was contradicting her before she finished speaking.

This little man had a temper: she could see that; he had greeted her in Irish when she entered and because she could only grin foolishly in reply, she felt she had upset him. But this present anger that was making him change colours was unaccountable.

'But my brother has already – '

'He has *not* inherited it! Your grandmother, Winifred Sarah Lally, who was of more than sound mind, made her last will and testament in this room, in the chair you are sitting in, without fear or favour of anyone, without any influence being brought to bear on her wishes, without any third person being present, leaning over her shoulder!'

Her impulse was to start laughing but pins of light were coming at her out of his eyes.

'What have I done?' she wanted to say. 'But!' she said.

'He has not!' said the dlíodóir, Pádraig Ó Síadhail. 'I'm very well aware – Ms O'Toole! – that there are two wills, but – I can assure you! – this is her last one.' He held it up. And now he leaned forward and lowered his voice to show his resolve: 'And-I-shall-see-it executed, exactly, and-to-the-detail-of-its instructions, as I'm obliged to do, as-its-executor!'

'But he has stock on the farm already!'

'Then he'll take his stock *off* the farm – already!'

Why was this solicitor fighting Vera? Because he was another honest man. The church owed him money and in the absence of a belief in any political party he went out and learned Irish. He was

198

proud of his race but not of the present generation and when he discovered unprinciple it encouraged the neurotic in him.

'He shall have to quit the lands!' he said. 'He's in for the surprise of his life! We shall go to court if necessary!'

Instinctively, she reached out to take the document that he was holding up, as if by gaining possession of it she could control this new, alarming situation. He swatted it on to his desk: 'This is for the Probate Office!'

Any impulse to laugh was gone, the surprise in her eyes watered over and she lowered her head.

Pádraig Ó Síadhail saw her lower lip begin to move, he saw a tear fall down behind the other side of his desk and he knew that he had carried himself away. The next time he spoke to the tearful woman across from him, he would not call her Ms, a word he detested. He picked up the little bell on his desk and he shook it, gently.

The silent, late-middle-aged woman, who looked like him, who wore a tweed skirt of the same cloth as his suit, who let Vera in, came in. 'Dein cóip de seo, mais é do thoil é,' he said without looking at her, giving her the will. Make a copy of this, please. And she went out again.

'You are now entitled to the house and lands, Miss O'Toole. Mmm, my dear.'

'Did she come alone?' said Vera.

Vera was driving the road from Newcastle to Glenora village and her heart was broken. Her grandmother had travelled this road, alone, and in secret as far as she could manage it, two years ago.

'Sometimes it happens, Miss O'Toole. Old people having to make two wills. Mmm.'

Vera was arriving at the crossroads and her turning for Glenora. It was here that Mom would have got the bus.

'Did you know she could talk Irish? Mmm, she could!'

Tom had isolated Mom from her neighbours and made her

dependent on him. He brought her sweets. And he brought her to Grange to his solicitor and stood over her while she made out a will in his favour. Mom had died on the floor.

Vera liked the little man in the Donegal tweeds but she was hardly listening to a word he said any more while she waited for her copy of the will. He had become chatty. She wanted to be on the move. Terrific thoughts of panic were flying through her mind. This was Thursday evening. She had booked her flight for Monday morning: that was more than three days away. Something was telling her to get out sooner, change the flight if she could, get out now. Because if this volatile little man were to act now, say, to write a letter, would her family hear the news of her second inheritance before Monday, her escape day? What did she think? But what could they do to her?

'I have to go back to the States,' she said. 'Do whatever you have to do.'

'Go deí tú slán!' May you go safely, entire, perfectly.

Vera had to see Mom, to see-see-see, to 'see' her. Two years ago, Mom had walked this road, the four miles from her house to the crossroads back there, got the bus to Newcastle and, somehow, found her way to that man's office. Perhaps the bus stopped in the Old Corn Market and she asked someone to direct her to a solicitor's office? And Vera felt ashamed of her own fear. Tears hung before her eyes, caught in her eyelashes, top to bottom. She had to press them out. Some people said that Mom was fierce: did they not know how shy she was? The compass of Mom's life, with maybe a few exceptions, was no more than a seven or eight mile circle: half-blind, over eighty years of age, at the end of her days, she had done that journey to Newcastle.

She was approaching the house. Her house. Might she dare sleep in it tonight? No. Already there were a few weeds growing out of the thatch. And there were, probably, rats in it now. She did not slow down. But it could be a beautiful place to live. Oh, it could. And, Lord, she was weary of being the big white

Mama, so much flesh to be weighed by their eyes no less than in their hands.

Ten, twelve, fourteen young cattle – heifers? – heifers, were standing doing nothing in the next field. Tom's. Her field. The next field was Conneeley's. Mrs Conneeley was going into her yard as Vera passed by: she looked back without stopping and raised one of her buckets, though it was unlikely that she registered Vera or recognized the car. The cake in the white box on the back seat was for Mrs Conneeley.

The road twisted and around the bend, sitting in the hollow below her, was the village. The small stone church, the graveyard and Melody's. The sand crunched beneath the car, warming to the tyres. Vera pulled into the bay outside the church.

There was a summer's day like this one, when Vera was eight or nine, when she walked over the road to here with Mom, to climb this stone stile. Mom was carrying a concrete block, an ordinary builder's concrete block, on her hip. Her shawl was draped loosely down her body like a sash, half of it wound around her arm against the hard edges of the block. They walked this avenue of yews, poisonous to cattle, past the sandstone crosses in old Celtic designs and the granite headstones, and turned before they met the more modern ones in black and white and terrazzo, to the corner where Mom's husband was buried. The grave was unmarked.

Mom's husband. Vera knew nothing about him and, until that day, she found it impossible to think of him as her grandad. All she knew about him was in the brown photograph. He stood very erect in the brown photograph, in a brown suit that was too small for him because his wrists and the uppers of his boots were showing; heels together, toes out; the toes curled up a bit; and a waistcoat; the shirt had no collar but it was buttoned right up; his eyes were very pale, but maybe that was the photograph because so was his face; and one side of his hair stuck up, as if he could not flatten it. His right arm rested stiffly on a pedestal. He was tall, lean, very serious, and handsome, sort of, Vera thought;

but no moustache or that kind of thing; and he was very young. And how could that be a grandfather?

Then, that lovely day, Mom put down her shawl and she began to dig with her hands at the head of the grave to mark it. 'It's only an aul' hole,' she said. 'But they make mistakes, Vera, d'yeh know. It's getting crowded. There's manys the widow-woman knocking about, waiting to get in here. What in the next world would I do if they put another woman down on top of him before me?' Then she smiled up at Vera. The sun was on her face and it shone through her hair where her hair had become loosened. In that moment Vera put her standing beside the young man in the photograph and, in that moment, the young man became Vera's grandad.

Mom never talked about him, just as Vera would never talk about Wally the Swede to anyone.

The concrete block was gone but Vera knew she had found the right grave: the oblong of fresh green weeds; nothing else had been disturbed in this corner for years.

Vera began to weed the plot of land. Without her knowing it, her sense of danger disappeared. There was peace here.

A group of three people was moving along the main path towards the new part of the cemetery. Two brightly-dressed women and a man a step behind them, smiling, his head bowed. He was unmistakably of the area: his walk. The two women were laughing, bobbing their heads to each other until they touched; they each carried a wreath; there was an English sound over their original accents. They passed no notice of Vera; they did not see her.

'Aw, you're a great help to me entirely.' Vera used to weed the onions with Mom; walk astride the drills, laying the slits of potatoes, with the eyes up, Mom following with the spade, closing the drills; lock up the hens. 'And will you stay here with me always?' 'I will.' 'Will you?' 'I will.' 'Well, d'yeh know, it might be the best place for you after all.' Mom wasn't always joking.

'I won't forget you, Vera.'

Vera cleaned the grave, leaving the daisies and something, she thought, that just might turn out to be a poppy. Then she stepped into the mearing and picked handfuls of the long grass to wipe her hands. The trio she had observed earlier were returning to the main path from their end of the graveyard. The two women, now, were linking each other and walking in step with their heads down. They were wiping their eyes, but they were still kind of laughing also. The man – their brother? – with the farmer's walk, was, as before, a step behind them, the quiet smile on his face. Then one of the women slowed her step, almost stopped, to bow her head to Vera and to smile. Then they were gone.

Oh glorious day, glorious evening! Vera's gratitude of the woman's acknowledging her filled her to overflowing. She felt extraordinarily lucky. This was the place to be, it was wonderful to be alive. Then another stroke of luck. Her toe was touching something in the undergrowth and, even before she stooped down, she knew that what her toe was tracing was the concrete block. She retrieved it out of the grass and the overhanging brambles that grew out from the wall and, just as Mom had done it, she set it upright on the grave, to mark the end of something, life returned to an aul' hole.

'Now! Naked we came into the world.'

The sun was going down but its heat was still warm on her shoulders. Maybe, after all, she should go back to what she wanted to do originally: give the hotel to them. Could she afford it? If it could be done simply, she could. She lay on her back, her arms behind her head, her ankles crossed. She had the whole place to herself. And she watched the sky, going from blue to a scattered red until it gathered and became a plateau of yellow.

XV

THE FUTURE

Tom was given another chance of the place, that Thursday: he declined again to sign. Robert Carney was approached that night but he shook his head; he was approached a number of times in the following weeks and, though he always listened patiently, he always ended up by saying, 'I don't think so.' It was Miss Lamb, the short, strongly-built woman who enquired about the contents on the day of the auction, who bought it. A hundred and seventy-nine thousand, the lot. But, taking it from that Thursday, the day of the auction, the disposing of the hotel took seven months. Vera would be seven months gone at that stage, safely back in New York. Caitriona would have left Tom. Many things were to happen in the intervening period. The Greek would have been in and out of hospital with broken legs.

Tom declined to sign the contract because Vera had to be protected from herself and society had to be protected from Vera. She had nearly taken the nose off him, sure, in a trickie's door above in the Punjab; she had been discovered in a terrible state entirely, hanging out a window, and then she tried to seduce the lad who discovered her; she barricaded herself in the hotel, the Guards had to break the windows to get in and see how was she; her sister, a woman with six children, lost the temporary use of her arms because of Vera. That was just to mention a few things. Vera was morally insane. The family had to commit her to a mental home for treatment and take over the administration of her estate.

The procedure of involuntary committal was easily achieved. It happened about three thousand times a year. Most of the cases were women. Some of them deserved it; most were released within six months; some were kept in forever. Acting on the Mental Treatment Act, 1945, a GP's signature could do it.

So, when she returned to Grange that night she felt a chill. At first she thought it was because of lying for so long beside her grandmother's grave, or it was because the night had turned cold and she had spent maybe an hour in Conneeley's yard and out-houses, talking to Mrs Conneeley before they went in to drink tea and eat the cake. But when she saw the police car waiting on the Square with its lights switched off, she knew it was something else. And when she got out of her car to go into the hotel and heard the doors of the police car opening and slamming behind her, she knew she was in trouble and that only luck could save her. One of them held out his hand for her keys and she gave them to him. To offer any kind of struggle or resistance would be a waste of time and energy, just as she knew that it would be unwise. And they drove her away.

Vera, though, was lucky. She did everything she was told and after three days, when the consultant psychiatrist got round to seeing her, he wrote on his report – a kind of certificate – 'inappropriate', ie, that retaining Vera would be inappropriate; and he wrote it down that he did not consider her a threat to herself or to other people. And they let her out. He gave her a copy.

So, when she was returned on Sunday evening and found them – Tom, Marcia and Mary Jane – waiting to greet her in the lobby of the hotel, it is not remarkable that, after the initial surprise of it, a thought that kept striking her was that she was the only certified sane person in the family.

The car circled the Square to drop her on the spot she had been lifted from on Thursday night. The hotel door was open and Father Billy Houlihan was standing in it. The Square was quiet. Vera noticed that there was no sign of her car.

Father Billy came to meet her. He took her two shoulders, bent his knees, looked up at her face. 'Wonderful!' he said. 'Vera!' Then, with one hand holding back an imaginary crowd to make a path for her, and the other almost-but-not-quite touching the small of her back, he ushered her in.

Caitriona was present also. She was sitting in a chair with one of her legs hanging over the arm of it, with her back to the door, and when Father Billy said, 'Look who's here!' she raised her glass of coke without looking around.

Tom, Marcia and Mary Jane were standing in a line. For a moment it looked as if Tom might clap. His face was full of enthusiasm and wonder. Marcia's, too, looked like bursting, but, in her case, it was with her usual kind of alarm. Mary Jane was first to break ranks. For all Mary Jane's head-wagging and grin, Vera knew that Mary Jane was fed up.

'How yeh?' said Mary Jane in a sort of mildly surprised or amused way, but, mainly, matter-of-fact. Then she said, 'How yeh!' shaking Vera's hand with the both of her own. And she stepped aside to give the next one a turn.

Marcia came forward to do the same but at the last moment she turned away, went behind Vera to hide her face, and could only trail her fingers on Vera's bottom.

'Lookit!' said Tom in a hoarse whisper. It was as much as he could do with the emotion. 'I couldn't be happier about anything!'

Vera went to him and shook his hand. She was afraid of them but she was determined not to put a foot wrong.

'Lovely hurling, girl!' said Father Billy, delighted.

'Up on your bike!' said the seated Caitriona, and it was strident.

Tom turned on her. But then he started laughing heartily, he nearly fell back over, pointing at her. His wife was a card.

There were two bottles of wine, opened, on the largest of the coffee tables and they sat down and drank a toast to themselves.

And they chatted.

Caitriona sat a little apart from them. Father Billy was drinking orange squash. There were cold meats, salads, glasses and soft drinks on the counter of reception. A section of the bar in the lounge bar had been opened in case Vera would like anything else. And someone had lit the fire to further cheer the occasion.

'Treasure?' said Tom at one stage. 'What are you doing?' calling to Caitriona who had left them, to drift quietly into the lounge bar.

No one knew the extent of Caitriona's unhappiness. On a Saturday, about a month after Vera had gone back to New York, she dressed her children in their best clothes and took them to church. Martina, seven and a half, had made her First Holy Communion and Caitriona told her to go to confession. Then, with Martina, Joe and Aisling in the back seat with their toys, she drove to Newcastle. She drove the car to the quays area and did not turn where she should have turned but kept straight on, over the ruts and the cobblestones towards the edge of the wharf to drive into the sea. It was Joe's shouting that stopped her. He saw what she was doing, got the door opened but could not jump: he was hanging over the road, his hands clinging to the door, his feet in the car.

'Nothing!' said Caitriona, returning to the lobby, smiling.

Father Billy had a private chat with Vera. Vera nodded thoughtfully to everything he said. He was a nice man, an innocent. There was a softness in his eyes that came towards you. People used him. Tom did in getting him to talk to her like this. The ginger colour of his hair was almost gone. Vera reckoned he was a secret body-builder, probably giving up on his exercises now or had given up: he was moving into his late fifties. She liked him.

He was not comfortable talking to her like this, though he told her it was his duty. She complimented him on the white silk scarf that he always wore, a half-inch showing inside his lapels and around his collar. In his pleasure he stood up, laughing, his chest expanded, and sat down again immediately. She laughed with him. He asked her if she knew Esther Williams, if she ever saw any of her pictures. Esther Williams was his favourite film star.

Dangerous When Wet. 'Where Esther has to swim the Channel. She's called Annie in the film – Annie Higgins, like, I think. I wonder was she meant to be Irish? But there was a French lassie in it too – Denise Darcel – and says Denise to Esther, "You sweem ze Channel and you mebbe win ze medal but that won't kip you warm at night." – Did you ever see it? You don't see much of her any more, I wonder why is that? Dangerous when wet, what!'

Later, Tom called her. 'Are you not having something to eat, Vera?'

'Yes!'

She joined him at the reception desk where the buffet was laid out. She was not hungry but she chewed the food methodically and ate everything that was on the plate.

'I didn't see my car outside?'

'Well, under the circumstances,' said Tom, 'yeh know, we thought it best to inform them.' He nodded his head at the keyboard, the rings of keys on hooks in reception. 'They're coming to collect it in the morning.'

He went to a corner and she knew by his shoulder-movement that he expected her to follow him. They stood together, their backs more or less to the room.

'How was it?' he said quietly, looking down at his plate.

'It was fine,' said Vera. It was horrific.

'Was it?' he said, concerned that it was, that it was fine.

'It was fine.'

He smiled sadly to himself and shook his head. He looked at her, hopeful of her understanding and so that she could see the tears in his eyes. Did she understand him? With downcast eyes she nodded her head slowly, three times.

'Well, d'you know what I'm going to ask you?' he said. And she didn't. 'Could we have a chat tomorrow?'

'What time?'

'Any flaming-well time that suits you, my lady!'

'Lunch?'

He could hardly contain his joy at the arrangement; he felt like killing a flaming calf. 'A bit of openness,' was all he wanted. He went to the middle of the room, halted, changed his mind about something, turned, went in the direction of the piano, but that did not appear to be enough either. He could not think what was enough to do for her, or for the others for that matter. He held up a finger – the doorbell had just rung – he would get back to it – and he went headlong for the door.

It was The Greek. And Finbar was walking away across the Square. The Greek had slept for the last three nights in an armchair up in Finbar's house. Tom had refused them entry to the hotel on Thursday night. But tonight was different: this was a night for reconciling families. Look at Marcia, the creature, sitting broken-hearted in there! And as to what he would do for Vera, Tom had that too! Any friend of his sister's was good enough for him, and he bounded into the Square after Finbar. Wasn't it raining, sure?

The Greek was a man who knew how to command a silence and, on entering, he looked neither left nor right but went straight to the mirror and stood there staring at himself.

'Mmm,' he said to his reflection, enigmatically.

He was unshaven; a three-day stubble, in fact.

Marcia made a little sound. Henry looked awful, he looked like a tramp; he was killing himself. Her hand, stretched out to him, rested on the air. She dared not to rise. Vera felt that The Greek had had enough; she was surprised at how old he looked. Caitriona got up so that he should have the armchair when he turned about. Of the four women present, only Mary Jane considered that he was putting it on, to get out of the situation: he had been home once in ten days.

The Greek sat down and began to move pieces on the table in front of him, clearing a space. Then, as if remembering something, he looked up and said, 'How are you!' three times, equally, in turn, to Mary Jane, Marcia and Vera. He did not appear to notice Caitriona: perhaps it was because she was standing. And he raised his hand to call a drink.

Father Billy was returning from the gents. The Greek watched him, puzzled. It was as if he thought that Father Billy was a barman. But then, working it out, he said to himself: 'He comes with garlic and a crucifix.'

Father Billy was puzzled. The gathering was silent: when he left it a minute ago it was jolly.

'Where is he?' said The Greek. Then, strangely, pointing at the ceiling, '*He!*' he whispered. Perhaps he was referring to God.

'I don't know what you mean, like,' said Father Billy, looking frightened.

But Tom was bringing in a reluctant Finbar at this stage. 'I hear you're one good man for a song, Finbar.'

'Man, Tomeen!' said Father Billy, relieved. 'How are you, Finbar boy!'

Tom moved around the table, drawing a chair behind him. 'Well, you're one gas man, Finbar,' he said, setting the chair beside Vera. 'Sit over here, my friend.'

He rubbed his hands together. Then, suddenly, he loosened his tie, opened his top button, took out his wallet and pitched it deftly on to the table.

'Does anyone here have any serious objections to a party?' he said.

The Greek was given whiskey, and Finbar, vodka.

'Lovely!' said The Greek with his eyes shut and his head back.

He was thinking of the future, the weeks – the months? – ahead; the lengths he would have to go, the tedium of it, to rid Marcia's pocket-searching mind of its suspicions and get her to resume playing decent ball with him. Nearly all his previous binges had occurred in Dublin or in Newcastle, his sexual sorties had been largely furtive, and she had given him a hard time: how would he convince her that he had not been sleeping with her sister?

He did not want to have to go in to St Pat's again to dry out. He was longing for his own bed. He was heartily sick of jobbing, of Vera and her hotel and auctioneers; he wanted no more truck with them. He wanted to get the household he commanded back to normal. And, as was the case following the other extra-marital, genital relationships, he was longing at this moment to have sex with his wife; it did that to him. There was comfort in sex in bed with Marcia. But, on the flimsiest of circumstantial evidence, she could carry a grudge to great lengths.

Yes, she was casting hopeful, bovine glances at him now, but wait until she got him home. She would feed him, bring him his lunch in bed, polish his shoes, collect the tray – she knocked on their bedroom door before entering! But she would not look at him. She went about her business – everything – like a big moping duck! And she would only do it backwards, she simply would not face him – you could not budge her – let alone sit on top of him, put pillows behind his head and give him the breast. She created such an atmosphere the children would not enter the bedroom on Sundays to walk on his back!

'After boredom, unfounded jealousy in a woman is the worst affliction a man has to endure!' he was forced to shout at her once. And he had seen Marcia's large face grow dark – *unknown to herself.* A clumsy woman could knife you in an emotion. Ah, but would she do it cleanly?

Tom was singing and playing the piano: something from 'The Lily of Killarney'.

'Lovely,' said The Greek, still with his eyes shut. 'Myles, a peasant, who is passing at the time, sees Danny on the edge of the lake and, mistaking him for an otter, shoots him.'

Despite Tom's relentless efforts the party was refusing to – and did not – take off. Father Billy sat bright-eyed and alert but he was only waiting to do his party piece and get home. Finbar did not take the chair that Tom had set for him beside Vera, but drew a stool for himself and sat under The Greek. Marcia's eyes watched The Greek hopefully. Sometimes The Greek's eyes fell vacantly on Marcia, rested for a moment on her as if in a puzzled memory of who she might be; his quips were of his usual standard but did not have the usual energy; he could have been saying them to the wall. Caitriona was growing more cranky. Mary Jane's legs were stretched out, her chair was turned away from the table and she looked at the piano in the thoughtful way that people watch television; she said 'Thank you' without looking when her glass was filled up. Sociably, Vera was the politest of them.

'How is Declan, Mary Jane?'

'Holding the fort. We're open seven days a week.'

'Folks!' said Tom. He had finished his number. 'I had one very good reason for getting my humble piece out of the way first and I'll tell ye what it is: "Sea, oh the Sea", Father Billy!' He did not want to follow a man like Father Billy Houlihan, who was no mean organist.

'This is piss,' said Caitriona of her Coca-cola.

'The organ is a musical JCB,' said The Greek.

'Little Treasure?' said Tom to Caitriona, asking her to observe that his finger was up.

'Sedimentary, my dear Watson!' said Caitriona, banging down

her glass. 'Does any person here have any serious objections to my having a decent drink?'

She got her way.

Tom winked at Vera.

Finbar was having a feed.

'The sea, oh the sea, grá geal mo croí, long may it roll between England and me.' Father Billy began his medley. He played a jazzed accompaniment to his rendering of the ballad and then went on to sing and do similarly to 'Blue Moon' and 'Apple-Blossom Time'.

'Henry? I'm your wife,' said Marcia. 'Are you coming home?'

The night had ended. Father Billy had gone home an hour ago. The Greek got up and went out ahead of Marcia. Tom and Caitriona were going to give them a lift. Finbar was already outside, standing in the rain, a couple of yards down from the door. He did not want The Greek's missus to think that he was leading her husband astray. The Greek was well able to do that for himself. You couldn't trust them. But he was waiting on in any case, in case of anything.

Mary Jane came out, nodded to him, skipped to her car and drove off at speed. Then the others. Caitriona, on tiptoes, held Vera's neck in her two hands and kissed her on the mouth. 'I envy you,' she said.

Then, as Tom turned his car and drove them away, Finbar made shapes towards the Dublin Road, turning a couple of times and waving goodnight.

Vera called him back. 'I'll give you a lift.'

'What?'

'Come in a minute.' And when he did: 'Help yourself to anything,' she said, indicating the drinks, and she went upstairs.

She returned shortly with her bag and went into reception, where she put the keys of the hotel in an envelope and wrote on the envelope what they were. And she took her car keys.

'Take the bottle,' she said to Finbar. 'Take the whiskey, too.'

'What?'

'We'll go out the back way.'

Finbar did the porch doors for her and she drove the Merc out of the yard. Finbar got in beside her and they drove off. Up the Dublin Road, over the bridge, a right turn into the street of deserted railway houses, to find the New Estate, to pull up outside Finbar's. She left the engine running. At this time of night, thirteen days before, she had pulled up here.

'Do us a favour,' she said, giving him the envelope that contained the keys of the hotel. 'Drop these into Martin A. Costello's office tomorrow. He's my solicitor.' She had the money ready and she pressed it into his hand as she gave him a kiss. 'See yeh!' she said on a laugh, and she was gone.

.

Seven months later, as the sale of the hotel to Miss Lamb was being completed, Caitriona could not stand life with her husband any longer and she took herself and her children to live with her mother and father. Her mother welcomed her home; her father did not understand it, but he would get used to it.

Tom believed she would come back to him.

Mary Jane and Declan gave him twenty-one thousand for The Wool Stores.

Marcia suspected she was pregnant again. It would be her seventh child. Norman hoped that it would be a brother. Marcia was fonder than ever of her Henry and, in a perverse way, she was proud of what she thought he had tried to do.

The Greek, to be sure, often thought about suicide. Thought about it, theorized; he was philosophically inclined: 'the always open door'. He could enjoy the privacy of his own company, thinking of ways of killing himself, drowning himself in waters that were fresh, and suchlike. But he had no intention of doing it or, indeed, of damaging limb. Christ did it and much good it did him, or us! And where were the waters that were fresh with all the slurry that was about, and seepage from a land that was

214

drunk on 10:10:20? To be sure, he was in foul humour when it happened.

He was walking the ridge on the bank of the river when he spotted the round farmer coming out of a thicket and, turning to escape an encounter, he wrong-footed himself and fell, breaking his legs and damaging his ribs. He could have been killed. It was the round farmer that pulled him out of the river.

The curious thing about it was – quite, quite remarkable! – to relieve the tedium of his life with Marcia's prolonged, unyielding unforgivingness, he had for the three days before the accident been composing a suicide note in his mind. He found it such an interesting exercise that he began to draft it on paper to see what it would look like. Even if it had struck him that the note could be used to better his present life with Marcia, on the day he slipped and fell he certainly had no idea of how to get it past the test of her cunning and suspicious mind, subtly, in a credible way. The version she found, before he was discharged from hospital, read as follows:

Dearest Marcia,

By the time you read this I shall be no more. How can I explain what I do not understand myself? I am being unfaithful to you in going to sleep with death, but have no thought in your mind that I was ever – ever – unfaithful to you in life. All my love to Norman and the girls.

Love,

Henry

Finbar got an anonymous box in the post. It was a saxophone. It was such a beautiful object he couldn't touch it. He thought that it must have been Vera's idea, but he couldn't say. He became frightened that someone had made a mistake, that the Guards would come for it and he sold it and bought a pup, a right one.

And Vera was pregnant, heigh-ho! She was a rich woman. And she had her grandmother's twenty-six acres, three roods, nineteen perches. She would do up Mom's house and, before the new year was out, she would go home to live there with her child (and with the ashes of Wally the Swede to be scattered in her garden). Her child would be able to choose to be a citizen of Ireland or America. And if her child was a girl she would be called Winifred. And if her child was a boy he would be called Willie. But, boy or girl, she didn't care.

☐	That Bad Woman	Clare Boylan	£5.99
☐	The Cure	Carlo Gébler	£6.99
☐	The Glass Curtain	Carlo Gébler	£5.99
☐	Loving and Giving	Molly Keane	£6.99
☐	Good Behaviour	Molly Keane	£6.99
☐	Time After Time	Molly Keane	£6.99
☐	The Dork of Cork	Chet Raymo	£6.99

Abacus now offers an exciting range of quality titles by both established and new authors which can be ordered from the following address:

Little, Brown & Company (UK),
P.O. Box 11,
Falmouth,
Cornwall TR10 9EN.
Telephone No: 01326 317200
Fax No: 01326 317444
E-mail: books@barni.avel.co.uk

Payments can be made as follows: cheque, postal order (payable to Little, Brown and Company) or by credit cards, Visa/Access. Do not send cash or currency. UK customers and B.F.P.O. please allow £1.00 for postage and packing for the first book, plus 50p for the second book, plus 30p for each additional book up to a maximum charge of £3.00 (7 books plus). Overseas customers including Ireland, please allow £2.00 for the first book plus £1.00 for the second book, plus 50p for each additional book.

NAME (Block Letters) _____

ADDRESS _____

_____

_____

☐ I enclose my remittance for £ _____
☐ I wish to pay by Access/Visa Card

Number ☐☐☐☐☐☐☐☐☐☐☐☐☐☐☐☐

Card Expiry Date _____